Poets to Come

POETS to come! orators, singers, musicians to come!
Not to-day is to justify me and answer what I am for,
But you, a new brood, native, athletic, continental, greater than before known,
Arouse! for you must justify me.

I myself but write one or two indicative words for the future,
I but advance a moment only to wheel and hurry back in the darkness.
I am a man who, sauntering along without fully stopping, turns a casual look upon you and then averts his face,
Leaving it to you to prove and define it,
Expecting the main things from you.

Walt Whitman 1860

Poets to Come

Grand Champions
2003-2023

Walt Whitman

birthplace · state historic site · interpretive center

Copyright © 2024 Walt Whitman Birthplace
All rights reserved.

Published by Red Penguin Books

ISBN
Digital 978-1-63777-583-7
Print 978-1-63777-582-0

No part of this book may be reproduced in any form or by any electronic or mechanical means, including information storage and retrieval systems, without written permission from the author, except for the use of brief quotations in a book review.

All individual works are copyrighted to the writers.

September 2023

Dear Friends,

The Board of Trustees of the Walt Whitman Birthplace Association (WWBA) and I congratulate the student poets in this Whitmanesque anthology!

Walt Whitman looked forward to "a new brood" of poets and wrote: "I am a man who…turns a casual look upon you…Leaving it to you to prove and define it, / Expecting the main things from you." (*Poets To Come* 1871, WW)

To foster "new broods," in 1986, WWBA began holding an annual student poetry writing contest based on a theme taken from Walt's poetry. What began as a local Long Island contest now brings national and international participation! Our outreach attracts over 2,500 entries annually.

Students, grades 3-12, submit their poetry according to age-related categories with winners selected by a panel of local poets. This publication, *Poets to Come*, celebrates the 259 first-place winners from 2013 – 2023.

We invite you to step into Walt's world through the vision, images, and words of the student poets in this collection. Each student internalizes Whitman's poetic sentiments and creates a unique response shaped in their own free verse poetry. We honor the poets for their outstanding achievement, and we applaud their family and teachers who guided them in their creative endeavors.

Each year, the Board selects a nationally recognized poet as our Poet in Residence who officiates at the student award ceremony held in Spring under a tent on our grand lawn. The celebration draws over 350 family and friends. The Poets in Residence offer personal observations to the gathering about the craft of writing poetry and their names are included in this anthology. Additionally, they donate one of their poems to WWBA to print and sell as a Limited-edition Broadside of 100 signed copies to support our education programs. We greatly appreciate their support.

We also appreciate our local, national, and international support which helps us to fulfill our mission to preserve the legacy of America's great poet, Walt Whitman. As a non-profit organization, our success is linked to the generosity of individuals like you, who understand the importance of fostering the life of poetry. Please connect with us in person or virtually on our website: www.waltwhitman.org.

Let us all celebrate this "new brood" of poets and look forward together to new Poets to Come!

Sincerely,

Cynthia Shor,
Executive Director, Walt Whitman Birthplace Association
Walt Whitman Birthplace NY State Historic Site
Huntington, Long Island, NY 11746

Editor's note:

My name is Matthew Hamilton, and I organized and designed this anthology of student poetry while working as an intern for the Walt Whitman Birthplace Association (WWBA) in Summer 2022. I was selected through a competitive process to participate in the Jaggar Community Fellows program at Adelphi University in Garden City, NY.

As a Jaggar Fellow, I was sponsored by Adelphi and selected by WWBA to collaborate with them as I was entering my senior year.
The opportunity to create this book and to work at Walt Whitman Birthplace Association was a great experience. I am thankful to Walt Whitman Birthplace Association for giving me this opportunity.

Upon graduating from Adelphi as a proud member of the class of 2023, I hope to showcase my creativity and passion and pursue a professional career in graphic design. I have autism, so pursuing my goal for a Bachelor of Arts in graphic design with a minor in video game design has been very challenging for me. But with hard work, persistence, and support from my family, I have found the right career path. When I'm not busy with work or school, I draw, play video games, watch movies, read books, and swim.

I would like to thank Adelphi University & the Jaggar Community Fellows program, the WWBA Executive Director Cynthia Shor, the WWBA staff & interns, and my friends Jake Nerzig and Gerard Farrell who provided rides to and from the Birthplace and assisted me during my time there.

Founding Editor
Matthew Hamilton

Acknowledgements

Walt Whitman Birthplace Association (WWBA) thanks all the student poets in this anthology who sustain the spirit of Walt Whitman.

WWBA thanks the parents, teachers & mentors who foster poetry by teaching the value of words.

We offer gratitude to the Poets in Residence who serve to illuminate and fulfill the legacy of Walt Whitman, along with gratitude to the annual contest judges who read every poem and delight in celebrating the creative endeavors of the students.

We are grateful to Matthew Hamilton, founding editor who spent countless hours pulling together this voluminous poetry edition. We thank production editor Alyssa Abesamis and graphic designer Alana Abesamis.

We are beholden to Education Director Lisa Pulitzer and Poet Educator Linda Trott Dickman, and publisher Stephanie Larkin, for bringing this project to completion.

WWBA greatly thanks the staff who make it all happen so effortlessly and joyfully–the Curator, Administrator, Event & Media Director, Controller, the Tour Guides, Poetry Teachers, Art Teachers, Volunteers, Interns and Caretaker.

We extend our appreciation to grantors The Claire Friedlander Family Foundation, Humanities New York, NYS Council on the Arts, Huntington Arts Council, and Poets & Writers for their support of literature, literacy, and learners.

WWBA offers appreciation to the New York State Office of Parks, Recreation, and Historic Preservation with individual thanks going to Governor Kathy Hochul, Commissioner Eric Kulleseid and Long Island Regional Director George Gorman.

WWBA relies on the support of the members, donors, sponsors and business associates whose contributions sustain daily operations of the Whitman Birthplace State Historic Site.

Contents

Grand Champions 2003	2-10
Grand Champions 2004	11-16
Grand Champions 2005	17-24
Grand Champions 2006	25-30
Grand Champions 2007	31-37
Grand Champions 2008	38-43
Grand Champions 2009	44-50
Grand Champions 2010	51-56
Grand Champions 2011	57-62
Grand Champions 2012	63-69
Grand Champions 2013	70-77
Grand Champions 2014	78-86
Grand Champions 2015	87-94
Grand Champions 2016	95-102
Grand Champions 2017	103-109
Grand Champions 2018	110-118
Grand Champions 2019	119-128
Grand Champions 2020	129-136
Grand Champions 2021	137-144
Grand Champions 2022	145-152
Grand Champions 2023	153-170

Grand Champions

2003

"To Foreign Lands"

Poet-in-Residence: Samuel Menashe

Chase Brennick

WE

We means together,
We means happiness,
We means united.
That's what we are,
united together.

United means
sure of oursleves.
There's no doubt if tomorrow will come.
As we are united, we are
strong.

Two hundred-twenty seven years ago,
America was young.
Now,
it is old,
not frail,
but powerful,
like the sun,
or a king,
but no one rules.
We live without ruling.
America is us.
We are those who represent the beauty of our beloved country.

Micheal Seidel

The Road Through America

The road through America is always changing.
In New York City
Beautiful Skyscrapers grab heaven by the foot.
Noisy cars honk,
Sounding like a song.
People running,
Disoriented at times.
A beautiful city
Where Liberty stands holding a torch.
Only on the road through America.

Still Changing,
The road never ends.
Through Pennsylvania,
A state of mountain and woods.
Mount Pocono with noble importance.
Filled with trees, boulders of no similarity.
The woods of the state
With trees like houses to all creatures.
Only on the road through America.

Niagara Falls stands beautiful
And tall.
In America an Indescribable
Scent in the air.
America where a grand diversity
Stands freely, equally, and bravely.
Only on the road through America.

Ariana Hackenburg

America

Blue are her skies and green are her trees,
Golden are fields, and blue are her seas,

Ripe is her fruit, and rich is her soil,
And filled to the brim with citizens loyal.

Long are her fields, and wide are her plains,
Complete with every season, from harsh snows to rains.

All kinds of weather, showing in her sky
Wind, fog, and hail, coming from up high.

Deep are her valleys, and high mountains with snow caps,
Wide are her oceans that send out wavy laps.

An independent nation which holds her head up high
An economy that grows and drops, with happy tears, and mournful cries.

Her citizens, who celebrate what holiday they wish,
Enjoying Hanukkah's menorah, or a splendid Christmas dish.

A place that remembers her past, the important dates and times,
Her famous wars and her math, interesting poems, songs and rhymes.

Where people observe their freedoms, and choose them rightfully,
But a lot of times where choices are wrong, and through them people learn,
to see.

Where leaders fight to defend our country, alliances around,
And when she is in a time of need many friends are to be found.

America the great, young, powerful and strong
You have been here for short, but in your future, years are long.

Ariana Heckenburg, First Place, Category C, Grade 7, Teacher: Mrs. Aver, School: Our Lady Queen of Apostles, 2003

Kevin Ryan

American Heroes

They race in as we scramble out
Ascending the stairs in leaps and bounds.
Our faces express panic and fear;
Their eyes display none.

Two steps at a time we descend;
Three at a time they climb.

The fiery walls grow larger
The building is a ticking bomb.
It is only a matter of time.
Yet, no fear is with them.
Three at a time they climb.

The flames engulf all they encounter
Their hunger cannot be denied.
The stealthy smoke overpowers its victims
But three at a time they climb.

To these American heroes, nothing else matters
But the lives of those who are trapped.
To them, each life is a precious gem
Each - except their own.
Their own lives are secondary
At least for the moment, *all* is secondary -
Except for lives of fellow Americans.

We are carried on the shoulders
Of the American heroes.
Their eyes are filled with courage and pride.
Their bravery is insurmountable,
Their sacrifices unbelievable,
Their strentgh immeasurable.

One by one, we arrive safely.
Pure turmoil we have seen.
The flaming mass behind us,
uncertainty before us,
And a savior in between.
(Continued next page...)

Patriot embraces patriot.
Each survivor as lucky as the next
For the American heroes have no fear.
Only two things can stop these brave souls:
Victory
   or the tragic end.

The flames are on the verge of victory
But the battle is not complete.
The clock is ticking for those still inside.
Their lives are in the hands of the American heroes.

Two at a time we descend;
Three at a time they climb.

Diana DiPietro

The Song Of America (We, America)

Trees and skyscrapers,
grow from ground, and concrete,
to dance with the sun to the song of America.
Diverse cultures sing their songs,
creating and becoming,
one chorus, one voice,
singing the song of America.
Colors blend in a mosaic of freedom,
and become one being:
the song of America.
The pulse of life:
the heartbeat of earth,
drums the patriotic,
song of America.
The footsteps of soldiers,
march with their heads held high,
saluting to the song of America.
Wolves lean their heads back to face the moon,
and chant with whales in neighoring waters,
the Song of America.
Eagles fly over the American countryside,
to watch over America's children:
For we are a strong people, America!
Through trial, through tribulation,
We rise!
We, pillars of Strength!
We, writers. We, artists.
We, philosophical thinkers. We, open-minded believers.
We, striving to acheive!
We, wanderers. We, travelers,
upon this song of open road:
The song of America.
We, lovers of life.
We, carriers of heart.
We, hunters of truth.
We, miners of dream, and destiny.
We, America!
We, mothers.
We, fathers.
We, sons and daughters,
(Continued next page...)

friends, and foes.
We protagonists, and antagonists, in this unwritten forever story!
We, poets, and signers
of this song America!
We, creators of music and art.
We, makers of buildings.
We, manifesters of thought, time, and phantoms!
We, pupils, and preachers.
We, students, and teachers.
We, heroes. We, saviors.
We, workers.
We, talkers.
We, farmers, and ranchers.
We, patriots, and revolutionaries.
We changers, and makers.
We, America.
We: The song of America.
Where bears, and beavers
leave their dens, and safe havens,
to witness truth,
and rejoice,
in the song of America!
Where the rich, and the poor are one,
and money has no meaning.
In this song of America.
Where sunlight dances,
dawn until dusk,
to kiss the horizon,
and celebrate,
The song of America!
Where life and death,
rise and fall,
mix and mingle,
to become one,
in praise of,
The song of America!
Where God has many names, and many homes,
but one body of believers,
who come together to worship,
in the song of America!
Where languages of many,
nations, faces, and flags,
congregate in three colors,
(Continued next page...)

(Red, White, and Blue)
to sing in one tongue:
The song of America!
We, America!
A nation of plants and people,
Trees and towers,
Animals, and angels,
born from the loving flesh of earth.
Who conceives creation,
and births, every walk of life.
We are the song of America!

Grand Champions

2004

"Among the Multitude"

Poet-in-Residence:
Marvin Bell

Jonathan Farrell

I once had a friend

I once had a friend
    who helped me off the ground
      when I was hurt

I once had a friend
    who gave me his extra lunch money
      when I was ten cents short

I once had a friend
    who helped me study

I once had a friend who was cool

I once had a friend
    who gave all my secrets away

I once had a friend
    who bullied me

I once had a friend
    who told me an untrue story

I once had a friend who was a fool

I *used* to have a friend

Chris Halbohn

Friends Are Like.....

My friend is a star in the night sky glowing when I am dark.
        He lights me, shimmering in my heart & mind.

Like a window in a saddened room, we gaze together to a happier space.
        When we fight, the window of friendship breaks.
        Yet our friendship is the mending glue keeping us together.

Our Friendship is the ocean. We, the marine life
        living through rough waves & gentle currents.
        Driving together.

        Our friendship...always may it thrive.

Chris Halbohn, First Place, Category B, Grade 5, Teachers: Mrs. C. Udgeheuer, School: Levittown Memorial Education Center, 2004

Michelle Bowers

Friendship

Friendship, like a precious gift
Must be held onto
Forever.
Like blooming flowers
Scattered among the rolling, grassy meadows
it grows.
Friendship
A moon gleaming over gloomy waters
It lights up a lonely night
Giving way to morning light.
Crack of dawn
When we arise it's *always* there
To count on
To depend on
Friendship
A tender warmth
On Blistering cold days
Warms from head to toe
Like heat from a fire
Pouring from a hearth.
Friendship
A voice from within,
The tongue of the heart.

Michelle Bowers, First Place, Category C, Grade 7, Teacher: Ms. Cupola, School Berner Middle School, 2004

Jenny Choi

In the vast field of green...

In the vast field of green
Where roses, tulips, and dandelions
Dance in joy
Where I too can dance in joy
With the friend I have with me

Roses blooming in vibrant red
Tulips, dancing like snow
Dandelions sparkling in yellow
I, running like the mellow breeze
My friend, shining like the spring sun

In arm and arm we cross the field
Where nature greets us with joy
For they too have never seen such friendship
Among the multitudes

Laughing and tumbling over
Crying with joy and pride
To have a friend beside me
Like the deepening spring

Laura Raposo

It's midnight and the car's at 80...

It's midnight and the car's at 80 - gliding down the frequency like a rocket in flight
You look over at me to make sure I'm smiling - and I am
I roll the window open an inch to give us some air
I see your hand, out of the corner of my eye, slide across the radio to turn it off
We sit back and listen to the sound of the wind
Shooting along the side of the car, trying to catch us as we race past

At two we park next to a frozen lake
It's like time at a halt - this place once alive, now muted under the constant stars above
I feel you close your eyes and I close mine too
I see summertime playing on the screen of my eyelids
I wonder, what is it that you see before you fall asleep
We say nothing for a while - some old song is on real low now setting a backdrop for our ponderings

I open my eyes and realize it's three thirty
Your seat is fully back now, and you're gazing out through the sunroof at the sky above
You speak and your voice begins with uncertainty, like it's been days since you've used it -
"In dreams, nothing is ever questioned as impossible, until you're awake looking back on it"
It's true - in dreams we see people that aren't there, faces morph, our roles change, settings are altered, and all the rules are broken, yet never in dreams do we say, "This can't happen"
I didn't have a reply just then, because it's taken me weeks to fully realize what all this has meant

So many nights have flown in my dreams - I've lifted myself off the ground and sat on the air beneath my body
I've traveled to the depths of the universe
I've seen the faces of those I'll never really see
Maybe I'll never truly understand why dreams have no limits
But maybe I don't have to - maybe all I need is someone to make me wonder why.

Laura Raposo, First Place, Category E, Grade 12, Teacher: Mrs. Paulinski, School: Floral Park Memorial High School, 2004

Grand Champions

2005

"When I Heard the Learn'd Astronomer"

Poet-in-Residence:
Nikki Giovanni

Micheal Testa

I admire

The person I admire
is as nice as a chirping bird
eating bird seeds. She plays
with me whenever I want.
She plays whatever I want.

Even though she's 88 years old
She's fun as can be. I watch
game shows with her and we
guess what the answer is.
We play kerplunk. She jumps when
it pops.

Then we play slapjack. I
always win because I am very
fast. Then we play war. I win
because I always get the aces.
I'm sad when she goes to Foxwoods.
I miss her.

When we go out her jewelry
is so bright it seems like it's
talking! When we go out to eat
She lets me pick the restaurant
I pick a Chinese buffet.

She is my grandmother

Micheal Testa, First Place, Category A, Grade 3, Teacher: Mrs. Stine, School: The Laurel Hill School, 2005

Christine Brathwaite

Ruby Bridges

She was innocent.
The whistles didn't care.
She was black.
That made her guilty.

The president saw that they were
equal.

I saw that he was right,
that she was
innocent.

The judge ordered
her to go to a
whites-only
school.

All she could do was pray.

I could see that she was scared.

The whites formed a mob.

They insulted her,
Tried to her.

All she could do was pray.

Pray that God would forgive
those people who had
no idea.

No clue.

Not even the slightest thought,
about what they were doing.

She was alone, and all
she could do
was prey.

I watched as she walked,
slowly, to the whites-
only school.

I saw her lips move.

I saw her pary
right in the middle of
the crowd.

They were clueless;
frustrated.

Yet she forgave them.

I think it remarkable that she
could do such a thing,
after they had been
so cruel to her.

To her race.

Courageous is the only
word to describe
her actions.

Ruby Bridges was truly a hero.

Michelle Bowers

"Tangled in the Seafarer's Knot"

Tangled in the knot he gave me.
Tangled in his words.
Tangled like a spider's prey
Trapped
On a sticky web
Of silk
Never to escape,
Stuck.
Caught.
Doomed.

He took the braided string,
A piece of child's hair
Golden
In the light
And gracefully tied
Single loop,
Perfection.
A rushing roller coaster
Turned upside down
Soaring like a bird.
My hair
Blowing
With the howling wind
Like the pieces of string.

I, Silently,
Patiently,
Watch the seafarer
Me, my blank face
Staring into his white, tangled beard
Curling like foaming waves
The smell of the sea.
His nimble, gnarled fingers
Quickly
Tie the knots
So quick
I'm back

Back in the roller coaster
Clenching hard
To the bars
Afraid
I will fall
With every churning wave.

Only to be left
Hanging
From the strand of string once again.

Square knot, water knot, figure eight
An ice skater
Dancing across the frozen ground with
Whichever way
The string turns.

I'm trapped in the knots
Tangled in them.
Never to escape,
Stuck
Caught
Doomed.
Woven into the maze
Of golden string
A dark
Winding,
Turning road
Hidden amongst starlit trees
And darkened by looming shadows.
Olny hope to escape
Untying the knot he gave me.

So, there I sat,
Giving in.
Only hope.
Slowly untying the knot he gave me.

Brooke Wanlass

Rolling Thunder

How odd he looked in that emerald elf garb

A blur of speed striding swiftly before me.

Impossible to miss in that lead pack of runners

A special-needs athlete among a sea of marathoners-

They-lawyers, doctors, and teachers competing for medals to display at the club.

He smiled unbashedly, no hint of a grimace or difference.

Strange, I thought, they would call my friend "challanged."

And, I, moments before cursing the reality of my watch

Pitying myself for my aching quads and feet aflame

Was suddenly transformed, seeing for the first time that day

The glistening sunshine drenching the boats in the harbor.

Remembering encouraging words of my less able friend,

I could hear, at least, the lyrical hark.

Thomas Moll-Rocek

A Friendly Stranger Playing Scarecrow

By chance in a field
I came across a newfound friend,
thin arms astretch.
I took him by the hand
and felt his wrinkled skin
and music burst within my ears
like ripe fruit.

And when he smiled
his peasant smile,
I tasted earthy colors
and saw cannonades of sound
and time was thrilled to a halt.

And when I observed his eyes
like fish in a golden bowl,
bliss filled me
with cool spring breeze.

Grand Champions

2006

"Sea-Winds"

Poet-in-Residence:
Molly Peacock

The Wandering Wind

As I roam the Seven Seas I blow a breath of cool air,
In the midst of the ninth month of ealry times,
Little children look to sail their kites into the blue
    sky,
So sad I wasn't there to lift them up,
I was wandering the South, exhaling warm air,
Hearing the children's cries of disappointment,
I race up from South quickly and swiftly,
I long to play with the young boys and girls,
As it travel, I pick up speed,
Faster! Faster! Faster!
I cannot stop myself,
Going too fast, I howl to the children to warn them
    but they do not listen,
If I don't slow down, their fragile kites will not survive
    my fierce blows,
Arriving in the North, I slow my pace,
The children shout and jump happily,
My warm breeze allows them to fly their feather light
    kites,
I dance in the sky with them, enjoying thier company.

Krisann Marquart, First Place, Category A, Grade 4, Teacher: Mrs. Grubb, School: LMEC, 2006

Casey Morrone

What Makes The Waves Churn

I am what makes the waves churn.
I am the force the makes the tree branches quiver.
I am what tumbles across the hills like a running child.
I am a draft,
I am the wind.

I make the leaves on the trees rustle.
I can be a blissful breeze that blows and bats at the grass.
I am the refreshing air that cools you off.
I am a breeze,
I am the wind.

I am the invisible hand that pushes you away.
I can be part of a devastating storm that rips roofs off of houses.
I make you feel like you've been slapped in the face.
I am a gale,
I am the wind.

I am the breath of God breathing down on his people.
I am like torrents of rain when He's angry,
I am gentle like a baby's breath when He's pleased.
I am a zephyr,
I am the wind.

I can be so icy that I send chills down your spine.
Yet I can be so hot that it feels like you're in the the middle of a dessert.
But I can be a temperate temperature like water with no ice.
I am a gust,
I am the wind.

Bailey Kirkpatrick

Solace in the Untamable

Fly, gulls! Fly!
Wander in wholesome circles, in outstretched wings to span's content.
Rise, glassy seas from your depths!
Mighty and furious sea-waves roll gallantly to the shores.

Blow, wind! Blow!
Carry the noble-hearted sailer,
Let him be safe within the crow's nest atop the ship.
Her sails are taut in the gusts of whistling winds and the crew
      sends her onward.
Heave-ho brave men tending the ropes, bring her home!

And silent are the solemn drafts before the storm,
And silent is his voice as he grows old,
And silent are the winds as they carry his ashes over the world.
But life before the silence is as sweet as fresh fruit pressed against my lips.
(Have you felt my guilding hand on your back?
Perhaps you thought it was the touch of the wind...)

Ever so cold are the winds that push against you,
Ever so familiar this battle is becoming -
But fear not!
The wind is most capricious,
The wind is most famous for its sudden change of mind...

Over busy traffic-cities and roseate sunset-meadows the winds surely fly,
Over blistering hot sands of the Sahara and swampy still-water marshes of the coast,
Over duckweeds, willows, spruces, lilies, and maples,
Over the top of a fishing reel and through a retired man's gray thinning hairs,
Over the curvature of a baby carriage with a newborn nestled inside,
Over the red and white striped lighthouse that stands sentinel on the land before me
      as her circling light licks the salty air.

I watch the brave beacon guide all ships to port
      whether they are massive ships, or slender sloops,
Bobbing in the wild and rough blue sea and buffeted by the
      unyielding strength of the fist of a wave, they come to me.

Bailey Kirkpatrick, First Place, Category C, Grade 8, Teacher: Mr. Matovcik, School: North Country Road Middle School, 2006

Christina Daniel

Wanderer

Taking my wayward voyage around the world,
To linger awhile against the blades of grass.
Making invisible paths across a field,
To sing a soft melody among the tranquil creatures.
Lacing around firm trees,
To entangle a maiden's locks nearby.
Soaring to the blistering frost,
To swirl intricate snowflakes dancing around a wonder.
Elating toward the heavens,
To grasp the delicate clouds.
Racing into whipping choas,
To provoke seas into fury.
Brewing trouble within,
To form a death spiral of destruction.
Seeking a refuge,
To open my soul to the glistening stars above.
Begging to reveal,
To whisper secrets to the luminous moon.
Welcoming warmth of rays,
To play with pastels of light radiating from the sun.
Tiring from long terks,
To cascade down among the shadows below.
Retreating into exile,
To vanish with the sands of time.
Fading from existence,
To await a second coming.

Sean Doherty

Sea Winds

Oh sea winds, why do you tantalize me so?
O'er the water you come with sweet scent that calms my soul.
To sit and to smell thy lovely fragrance is to live life on a wing.
When you blow, I feel as though I am losing myself, as though I can fly away.
With every breaking wave I feel thy pressure grow stronger, stronger, stronger...

Oh sea winds, why do you tantalize me so?
To feel your cool breath upon my face,
It calms me, touches my heart, keeps me safe,
Just like that of a lover's embrace.
Your breath calls for me to join you in your wonderful palace over the sea
It calls for me to leave everything behind, to be along and free.

Oh sea winds, why do you tantalize me so?
Why do you call out to me to join you?
Why do you send the sweet scents of the sea to cloud my world?
Why do you numb my senses and cause my mind and heart to drift on fantasies and dreams of freedom?
What am I to you? Am I but bait on a line to lure others in, or am I the prize you seek?

Shall I join you now in the kingdom above the sea?
Shall I give into your tantalizations and leave my world behind?
Oh what a joy it would be, to leave everything behind and live a life on the sea,
Entangled in your beauty and grace; take over me please; take me away.
Take me and let me forever be in a place where I can fly free; where I can lose myself, where I can be and only just be...

Oh sea winds, why have you tantalized me?

Grand Champions

2007

"The Gathering"

Poet-in-Residence: David Wagoner

MaryKate DiNorcia

Gathering Dreams

I gather my thoughts and dreams for the world,
If it were all up to me,
The poor wouldn't be poor - they would have riches,
The greedy would share, the mean would be kind,
The deaf would hear the sound of sweet carols being
sung softly,
The blind would see the colors of the sun, and farmers,
miners, and factory workers would all have
breaks to regain their strength.
Everyone would be treated equally,
Together the poeple of the world would gather in
Harmony.
These are my thoughts and dreams that I gather
in my mind.

Jordan Sagarino/ Josh Spiegel

Gathering Thoughts

      I gather thoughts in the day and in the night. I dream about notions every day without even knowing. I gather images every second of the day. Some are happy, some are sad, some are silly or mad;

      I gather ideas of what to do and what to say throughout the day. My thoughts don't fade away at night. They last forever in the corners of my mind. Until I need them again.

I Gather Words

I gather words,
I gather thoughts,
I gather beliefs,
My thoughts are not like yours,
My thoughts,
Are not mine,
I did not,
Create them,
I gathered them,
I made them my own,
I adapted them,
I changed,
Mixed,
And started a new thought,
I don't call them mine,
For they are everyone's,
I do not think that if you gathered what I have,
You would think differently from yourself,
From me,
From the World.

Jordan Sagarino, First Place, Category B, Grade 6, Age 11, Teacher: Mrs. Pajkowski, Smithtown Christian School, 2007

Josh Spiegel, First Place, Category B, Grade 6, Age 12, Teacher: Mrs. McNamara, School: Saw Mill Road School, 2007

Ryan De Vito

New York Gathering

The silver snow falls as I ski from the summit of Whiteface in silence; the only sound is that of my skis carving out the snow,
The cool waters of the Saint Lawrence push us downstream in our white-water kayak,
The soft sand is shoveled on me by children who have come ashore from their sailboat moored in Sagaponack.
Do you know the place I speak of?

I have seen New York, perhaps the most picturesque state, the microcosm of this great nation.
I have seen the most gorgeous flowers and trees grow in this great state; the red roses, the colorful carnations of purples and blues, the tall evergreens of the Adirondacks.
I look on to the stunning shales and sandstones which are sheltered by the plants of all kinds.

The wind whispers in the willows on a warm summer day;
The sky is azure blue and rarely a cloud passes over;
The steep hill-slopes can be seen in the distance;
The family's old Ford pulls into the driveway and is followed by a few more.
The family gathers together to celebrate the independence of their country.

I hear the school children play, the distant laughter among friends, the light breathing of runners as they pass.
Can you not hear these sounds that are all around us?

I see children eating strawberry ice creams and socializing among friends on the stone walls by the schools,
The heated pursuits on the highway as the panicked criminals push their way through the traffic in their cars,
The many immigrants as they wait on the road-side for an oppurtunity to work for even the smallest amount of money,
The musically-gifted men and women who play a superb string quartet in the small town park
    (Can you hear the marvelous concertos they are playing on their cellos and violins?)

The school calls early in the morning;
I peer out of my window to see the neighorhood's children going out to play in the newly fallen snow.

The seamen take their small schooners through the Shinnecock Canal and out to the Atlantic;
I can see the small nets and the new salt-water fishing rods tied loosly to the stern of their ships.

The sun rises over ther vineyards in Bridgehampton;
I can see the men set out to to harvest the grapes to make thier fine wines similar to chardonnay.

I hike slowly through a mountain pass in the Adirondacks where nature's creatures and plants gether.
A family of deer are curious, (Could it be that they've seen a being like myself before?)
I sit in a field of wild lilac and lavender and open my pack to eat my lunch.
The foxes come close to me as I eat, as do the birds and squirrels;
The frogs from a nearby pond croak and fish flounder quickly out of the water;
The deer edge slowly near to me and lie down next to me in the field;
The rabbits stick their little noses into my pack to see what they can find.
                                    (continued)

Then I rise and find that I am so much taller, larger than these animals that surround me;
They must notice the same, for they scurry of into the fields and into the thicket.

I pull my bike along-side a boy in the park, for there is a crowd,
I wonder what they could be watching and I move closer to the center of the crowd, leaving my bike
	behind.

I now see and hear the brilliants sounds of the saxophonist's raspy tenor saxophone.

The family gathers to greet their eldest son as he returns home fighting in the war in Iraq;
At the same time, tears fill the eyes of a mother and father as they say their goodbyes to their son, who was asked to fight in the war in Afghanistan. (I give you these details beacuse I have seen men and women alike leave their families to fight for the greater good of our great country.)

I join the people of Albany as they gather along Main Street to welcome the governor of the state;
I can see the podium at which the governor will make his speech for his re-election in the following month;
I seem to be singled out in the great mass of people, for I feel as though the politician cares especially about my vote in the counting election.

The sun sets as I sit among my gathered friends on the crabgrass and carnations that edge the
	Susquehanna River,
I enjoy looking onto the spectacular evergreens that cover the Catskills, which surround me;
I notice every detail of the flowers in front of me and examine the tiger lillies a few feet away.
I notice now like the river, glorious and perfect, the bond between my gathered friends and me grows stronger every day.

Brandon Dove

The Riot

There they are again,
Slowly gathering at the wall.
They all do this often-
Trying to break it down, I suppose.

Back in the day when man was child
The thoughts and feelings freely flew inside and out of him.
But man tends to hide his feelings as he grows old and creates a wall-
Feelings and Thoughts don't enjoy being closed up inside walls.

There goes Anger, thrashing about.
Over there is Sadness, beginning to pout.
They all riot and knock up against the Wall,
Yet nothing budges nor answers.

There they are again,
Gathered and protesting,
Because Feelings and Thoughts are constantly born,
Yet the Wall that holds them doesn't ever change.

So at the end of the day,
The Feelings and Thoughts return home,
To their community of isolation inside of the Wall
That exist in man's mind.

I don't know what caused the Wall,
Be it a tragedy or some sort of disease.
But man must learn for himself that he must open up
Before this wall will begin to decompose.

Until then Isolation stands strong and tall
And the gathering will persist.
Yes, they'll be there again,
Struggling to break through.

Jonathan Andrews

" I'm just beginning my thirteenth or fifteenth book,"

depending on whether or not you count
the other two pending collections of poetry,
thick tablets on which are
several years of
suffering, love requited and sketches of shadows
from my car window,
nine o'clock on a Thursday evening.

Most of it people will never read.
I dont' really plan to return to it either.

It is the accumulation of three years
of my lack of understanding, to be followed
only by the aging and deterioration of a disturbed mind,
reflected in the looking glass of ink and pen.

Yet all of it seems part of some larger footnote,
another book, another name,
another endless chronicle of some measured parcel of time.

The years be damned by eternity
A measurement boundless and incomprehensible.

And because of this I never was at all.
Where then could I place myself in the
portrait of time, if I have nowhere to come from?

Grand Champions

2008

"The Crossing"

Poet-in-Residence:
Alicia Ostriker

Claire McDonnell

FERRYBOAT CROSSING

above the waves above the foam
different speeches many faces
in the jungle of a ferryboat
hearing the foghorn loud and low
feeling the water spray upon my skin
crossing the Long Island Sound
trying to get to Connecticut
the golden sun breaking through
all of the clouds pearly and white
just me by myself all alone
standing in the midst
of a sea of people
in a voyaging ferryboat

Allison Wallace

So Close to Freedom

As the moon and the stars come out,
So do us runaway slaves.
We turn under the thick blanket of the night.

Dawn is neat.
We must go hide,
Up a tree,
In a bush,
In a field.

The bark of the Master's dogs,
His foul words pierce my ears.
Just like the Master's whip on my back,
I hear a gun shot.
My heart stops,
They leave empty handed.

Under the quilt of the night,
We turn.
The blackness wraps around me like a shawl.
The eyes of others as big as moons.
No, not my eyes,
My eyes are as still as glass

I see a quilt,
It must be a sign.
I knock on the door hoping I am right.
A man's thick, heavy voice says "Who's there?"
I answer in a shaky voice,
"A friend of a friend."
The door swings open as if we are old friends

The morning is dark,
We leave in our director's wagon,
Under the sacks of things to bring to the market.
The wooden boards are cold,
The hay pricks my skin.

Days turn into nights,
The road to freedom is a long twisting road,
But finally we make it to Canada.

I turn in the sun and sing,
Free at last, free at last,
Finally

Allison Wallace, First Place, Category B, Grade 5, Teacher: Mrs. Marie Mansen, School: Minnesauke School, 2008

Alec Weinstein

Spring in Retrospect

Magnolia
Erupted in crème
And rosy hues
The air
Redolent
With its
Intoxicating
Aroma
Her auburn hair
Rustled
In the
May breeze
As I sat
Immersed in
Hemingway's prose
I watched
As she
Frolicked
In the
River
On this joyous
Spring day
Her laughter
Pulled me
From the shade
To the placid
Waters
I crossed
Through the
Verdure
Into the
Serene
Stream
We dove
For the myriad
Fish
That fluttered
Over the
River stones
Under the noon-day sun

Now, engulfed
In the bleak
And somber
Days of autumn
I will always remember
That jubilant
Spring day
When Bailey and I
Went a-river-crossing.

Linda Liu

Needlework

Weave a pattern, a design -

Guide the silken threads!

Through the dark tunnels

Through the caves

Through the sparks and the failed fires,

Which dampen with each storm.

Be the gentle stream sleeping between the mountains,

Be the artificial trail winding in the forest,

Be the fibrous veins flowing within the leaf,

Be the gossamer thread passing through the needle's hollow.

Seek the sun but follow the moonlit path,

Walk on weightlessness to cross and

Spin in fearlessness to create, to make, to craft.

And once what you seek is found

Stand back

Admire your stitches

In life's embroidery.

Amy Ross

Saturday Mornings

At 7:40 the doors slide shut
It pulls me away
Tired eyes, headphones in my ears
Dozing off, finally awaking as we enter the dark tunnel to our destination

    Doors open
    Moving floods of people on a mission come pouring out
    I, too, am one of these people
    Clutching my portfolio close to me

        As the escalator carries me up, gusts of cold air try to carry me down
        Little by little, as the escalator inches up
        The more I can see that greatest city in the world
        Quickly pushed into the rushed life of billions

    Many distinct faces pass me
    Homeless, struggling for life
    Disturbed, caught in the city's wrath, without any hope
    Working class, five days a week, hustling
    Rich and Famous, photo shoots, high end stores

    I've been here so many times before
    Yet I still I maintain tourist tendencies

Pinching myself as I stand in front of my possible future
Showing my I.D. card, taking up the elevator, sitting down in my seat
Discussing and drawing, learning and growing…

        I do this every Saturday

Amy Ross, First Place, Category E, Grade 12, Teacher: Mr. Patrick Cauchi, School: Longwood Sr. High School, 2008

Grand Champions

2009

"Metaphor for For Myself"

Poet-in-Residence:
X.J. Kennedy

Isabelle Scott

Water

A gentle stream
Moving quickly
Gliding on little fish-like skates

Swirling fast
Round and round it goes
A never-ending whirlpool of otter laughs

I roar
I crash
I wet strange creatures
With features unseen and...skin.
A gravely voiced ocean
Whipsering and beckoning to you curiously

A calm soothing lake
Its laziness slides off on to you
And you are - Relaxed

All these things am I?
Yes. Because I am
Water

Isabelle Scott, First Place, Category A, Grade 4, Teacher: Mrs. Wasner, School: Laurel Hill School, 2009

Chris Kayel

The Lighting Like Cheetah

The lightning like cheetah,
Swiftly jumping out if its hiding bush going after its prey,
Catching the gazelle in the hot Sahara Desert.
It's happy that it got the last gazelle in the field.
Goes running off to eat its prey.

I just hit the ball into centerfield with bases loaded.
I start running as fast as I can to first base.
I make it to first and I start running to second base,
I make it to second and start going to third.
I made it to third and start running to home.
I make it to home plate before the throw.
We win! Everyone is jumping on me excited.
We won the game!

Arielle Heiman

Ode to the Moon

A silver coin, hanging gently on the dark wall of night
A gentle reminder, like a mother's kiss
That all will be alright,
Always there to light up my path,
Showing me the way through my gardened childhood.

One day I will be the one, watching over one of my own,
Hanging in a star-studded evening,
The wind whistling a lullaby
Looking, with ever-watchful eyes
At a child in crib blessed with the chilled nights beauty.

Dylan DeFeo

I, the Note

The musical note
Incarcerated in a 5 pronged prison
An ink-clad circle
Visually meaningless
And monochrome depression

I, locked in these 4 walls
Stuck to follow the regimen
And schedules
To follow the rules
And be a pawn of teachers and parents

The musical note, though barely
Significant as lives are lived
Is very special indeed
Place the wooden, brass, metal
Tool in the right hands
It becomes a wonderful figment of sound
And music

I, blending in with the crowd and daily bustle
Am also very special
I put my mind tool to work
I motion my hand and write
And draw
And make beautiful art

The note and I meet at once
Closing day of drudgery
And my tool to awake it
Reaches my lips
Exhaling tiredly and confidently
The note shouts
Long, loud clear.
I smile. We are one,
And we are art.

Dylan Defeo, First Place, Category D, Grade 9, Teacher: Ms. Fearon, School: Northport High School, 2009

Erica Ciringione

Reflections

I am a reflection
Of my father
The days of fear, the days of sorrow.
I am a reflection,
The doctors rushing in to take the pain away.
I am reflection,
The one last time I ever got to hold your hand.
The one last time I cried for you to come home.
I'm pained to say I forget what you look like, what you smell like,
The sound of your voice.

I see your picture; I read the poem you wrote me.
I smile,
Smile because I know you're here,
Smile because I fell my heart, in my dreams.
I am your daughter, I am your blood.
I am a reflection of you.

I am a mirror of the past.
I cry for you, Mom.
I cry for the pain you held within,
The tears you couldn't cry.
The words you left unspoken.
I remember you from childhood Mom.
You never put your glass down,
You never stopped to think.
I hope that you remember Mom,
All the times that I was scared,
All the times you needed help,
To come and pick you from the ground
As you lay there with silent movement.

(continued)

I want you to be proud of me Mom
For all the things I've done.
For every time I cried for you,
For every time I begged to come home.
I want you to remember me Mom.
Remember I am always here.
Remember the times I made you laugh
I will always hold that true.

Although the past is shattered
With broken memories and tears,
I can put the pieces back together
Through my flaws and through my fears.
Although I am a reflection,
Or a mirror of my past,
I am the daughter of my Mom and Dad,
The sister of my best friend.
I am not the girl you thought I was
But the reflection within myself.

Grand Champions

2010

"That Music Always Round Me"

Poet-in-Residence:
Mark Doty

Jack Niven

One Big Concert

I can hear the sounds around me, it's is music to my ears

The hustle and bustle of Perm Station is like Stevie Wonder's jazz music right in my face...... it's a mind boggling experience

I seems to be neeeeeeeeeeeeeeeeeeeeeeeeeeeeever ending

All the talk like piano forte

I need the bustle, I need sounds, honking, screeching of tires,
the "Hi, hey, what's up?"... everything

Nothing can stop me from listening and following
along with the beat, it's a thrill

All the different languages accents - amazing like a whole new song

This concert inspires me to speak out

I learn from listening to all the talk of Grand Central,

listening to the different languages

I love the sounds - the pings the pangs the ring ring ring the ding dong
the click the clock - all of these

noises are amazing... zoooooooooooooooooooom goes my mind

bing, zooooooom

Jack Niven, First Place, Category A, Grade 4, Teacher: Miss Field, School: The Green Vale School, 2010

Trevor Kennedy

The Beach's Symphony

Have you ever been to the beach by yourself?
The beach's breeze swirls through me; the breeze carries the sand from the
 hills of the dunes into the ocean's water.
Relax, floating in the ocean's arms, while gently the sand whispers,
 "Whoosh-swish-woo."
The waves grab the sand with a light crash.
The sunlight swirls, a mixture of oranges, reds, and yellows.
The sun is gazing at me, then a grand pause.
Silence...The waves break the ice with a whoosh then a crash into the
 sand.
LOOK! The winds sing the harmony, while the waves' peaceful crashes take
 the melody.
Working together, they combine, making a calm, warm symphony.
There is a soft vibrato in the breeze, and then the tempo rises.
The ocean tide turns gently, a serene scenario, everything is calm, the palm
 trees give us shade, a helping hand.
Lying on my back now, the sand is woven silk.
My eyes are closing in a rhythm, closed 1 2 3, open 1 2 3, closed 1 2 3,
 open.
Finally they are closed, sleepily dazed, my feet covered in the warm sand
 blanket.
A dreamer now, sound asleep, dreaming.

Justin DiBennardo

The Ocean's Symphony

The ocean, a kaleidoscope of color, sound, and wonder,
Waking my senses to hear the maritime music all around me.

Seagulls screech in the misty light of dawn,
Gliding freely over the aqua-blue waves.

Spectacular, swirling spheres of silver-sided fish,
Hover over the unfathomable depths of the deep.

From far away, the sea echoes the tranquil din
Of the melodious songs of the majestic whales.

Colorful coral reefs shimmer in the midnight light of the moon,
'Neath the slumberous lapping waves.

Seals dart daringly through the murky shallows,
Evading the sharks that persevere to devour them.

Jungles of jellyfish bob up and down with gentle currents,
Supporting their persistent efforts to stay afloat.

The ocean, its boundless brilliance invades my soul,
Stirring my passion for the maritime music all around me.

Tiffany Chang

Spanish Guitar

While walking the street of a village in Spain
A melody, soft and clear,
Drifts through the air above the lane.
Curious, you follow your ears.

You find a man sitting upon a crate,
A guitar perched on his knee.
The notes flowing from his fingertips create
Delectable harmonies.

You watch him play, your eyes aglow,
Not a single word does he say.
Yet you hear the tale of a love long ago,
One that had faded with the day.

You feel the steps of a forgotten dance
And smell the fleeting fragrance of roses.
You're caught in a mystical trance
By the melody he composes.

Yet there's no happy end to this affair,
In his heart there remains a scar.
He ends his piece with a melancholy air,
A tear falling upon his guitar.

Emily Sweetman

Wet Sand

The current sways to the tempo of the breeze.
Rythmically stroking the sea's silk surface
Like a bow soars over the strings tracing delicate shades of sound
Ripples whisper teasing notes
Rolling waves hum and dance in tune
Sharp staccato scent of salt
Rushing to the senses like lyrical ecstasy
Thin slivers of silver clouds reflect a duet upon the pallid depths
Hues of gold play on the sun soaked shores as skilled fingers play on ivory keys
Coast of oyster shells composed in harmony with pearls
Water surges up sand to meet and with swelling symphonies retreat
High reverberating pitches of gulls' calls
Pulse of wings beating at leisure
Wild flowers ring in a range of dulcet chords
A melodious bouquet, a multicolored arrangement
Inspiration from creation
Nature's jewels of tone rushing in air
Making human voices teeter to a silence

Emily Sweetman, First Place, Category E, Grade 12, Teacher: Mr. Patrick Cauchi, School: Longwood Senior High School, 2010

Grand Champions

2011

"All Gather and All Harvest"

Poet-in-Residence:
C.K. Williams

Food Feelings

Charming chicken soup on a gloomy rainy afternonn
savory sweet bringing joy to my day.

Pleasing oatmeal on a frigid weary morning
warm like an old friend.

Cheerful sweet ice cream on a roasting summer's day
like an icy wave in my mouth
sweet splendid taste on the tip of my tongue.

Merry mints on a torrid summer's day.

Food that comforts me.

Food Around the World

Millions of smells and exotic odors waft through my nose,
And suddenly I'm in Italy.
A waiter sets down a plate of bread with sauce on the side in front of me.
I take a bite and let the delicious Italian food find its way to my stomach -
Is that some spice in the meatballs?
I grab a bite of gelato before I am whisked to India
Where I take a bowl of curry,
The spice burns my tongue, but I like it.
My vision blurs,
And then I see sombreros.
In my hand is plate holding a yummy taco
Filled with more meat and spice.
I am in the streets of Mexico
Where girls dancy in fancy dresses
And children beat piñatas.
I smile at the taste of hot enchiladas
The man at the taco shop has a British accent;
He spins me a story from when he lived in England -
Fish n' chips, they called it,
Salty fries and bland codfish,
The perfect combination to satisfy me as I slowly drift to sleep
dreaming of one thing: Food.

Dorothy Yu

All Gather and All Harvest

As I climbed up the ladder,
The trees seemed endless
I closed my eyes
And relished the autumn wind
I stole a glance
At my basket
It was not yet full, reminding me
Of what I came here to do
I tugged at the apple
Breaking it free from its maker
It was impossibly shiny,
As red as Snow White's
I climbed down,
Gently placing it in the basket
I looked down the tree line
There was a long way to go.

Tristan Turnier-Baez

A Plethora of Temptation

I taste tropical fruit-flavored ice and am brought back to hearing the sounds of women yelling to one another. I smell truck exhaust and burning wood, and am brought back to my loose and yellow colored country.
The brewing espresso intruding upon my nose, and the cold air in my face let me know that I have arrived home, and I am in familiar territory.
I eat the Mentos, and as their mint sensation both burns and cools my tongue, I marvel at this strange euphoria, and continue to eat.
As I sit before the large abundance of food on my plate I ponder what meal an impoverished farmer would eat, and I sit in somber thought for a moment.
In this strange, far away tropical island, I am temporarily brought home when I see a Domino's pizza shop among brightly colored trucks and street vendors.
In the damp basement, lit only by a table lamp my fear of the dark subsided when presented with a warm chewy Cinnabon.
While typing, I eat a fresh navel orange. Its multiple little bulbs of tangy juice quench my thirst and satisfy my hunger.
In a restuarant, a wandering vagrant savors his slice of pizza. This will possibly be his only meal, yet he is content.
At breakfast I taste the crackled smoky taste of bacon, and I smell sulfuric, buttery aroma of eggs. This awakes me from my dreamlike state.
I am the chicken in the fields. As the blue sun sets in the west, I begin to ruffle my feathers to keep warm. This is a normal night to me, but soon enough I will become one with a human.
I am a man biting into a quesadilla and it pops as I do. It explodes with spicy cheese chicken flavor. I am brought back to the summers of my younger days.
The peppery beef jerky tickles my throat, but warms my cheeks as I am reminded of my childhood.
As I start to chew the Orbit spearmint gum, a cool honey-like taste fills my mouth and nose and I get reminded of seventh grade, Purell, and long days of tests.
The sweet, coconut candy makes me think of someone else eating it on a busy, breeze-caressed street.
The spicy and pungent oder of garlic and onion frying in oil tickles my nose and is a reminder to me that dinner is being prepared.
As I lift a peach to my nose, the tangy smell rolls my eyes into my head and I bite.
I will never forget my first taste of pumpkin soup. Though smooth and sweet, it was gritty and spicy, and that flavor is like no other.
I am the frustrated and tempted dieter, and as I try to discipline myself against the cold pizza, thoughts of indulgence and self-loathing race though my head. Reluctantly, I give in.

Tristan Turnier-Baez, First Place, Category D, Grade 10, Lawrence Woodmere Academy, Ms. Laura Maffei, 2011

Terrence Sweeney

Food

The car is running, it's twenty to four
The people are cheering, as I walk in the door
I walk to the grill, as a conductor greets his orchestra
I see my clear fresh oil, my stainless steel spatula
Knowing that I will be in control this evening

My gloves are clear plastic, the conductor's are white
We both get started, knowing it can be a long night
The grill starts to heat, like a hot summer's day
The meat starts to cook, there will be no time for play
Angus and doubles, Big Mac to go
No time to stop until it gets slow

Nuggets and fries cooking in the vat
The pressure is on, like a player up at bat
As I look at the time, my shift is almost over
I finally get to eat the fruits of my labor
Golden fries, so crispy and salty
Big Macs are so tender and juicy
I bow to the grill, my job is done
Some call it work, I call it fun

Terrence Sweeney, First Place, Category E, Grade 11, Longwood High School, Mr. Dirfetus, 2011

Grand Champions

2012

"I Hear America Singing"

Poet-in-Residence:
Martin Espada

I Hear History Singing the History

Those historians, each one singing Yankee Doodle.

Elvis Presley singing as he rocks out.

George Washington singing as he fights
Or singing The Declaration of Independence.

John Glenn singing as he watches space,
Abe Lincoln as he tries to stop slavery.

Thomes Jefferson singing as he writes freedom.

I hear history, singing the history

With his feather pen, Ben Franklin
Singing on the hard ground flying a kite.

The Wright Brothers singing as they create
the first plane in the woods.

John Adams' song, Franklin Roosevelt
Singing during WW2 in his office.

The sweet song of Henry Ford, or of
The nice John Q. Adams singing or Teddy
Roosevelt running and singing.

Elena Metcalf

Dreams of Music

I tune my ears to the world when I am tired of the radio
Beautiful music floods my ears; I leap up and run outside to enjoy the chorus of life.
I jump out the door and run down the street.
My feet are instruments, drumming on the ground.
A little boy and girl sing of the wind rushing through their hair as they twirl.
The butcher belts out a tune as his knife thuds onto the cutting board.
The flowers seem as if they are wafting a song into the air
Instead of their wondrous aroma.
Sing! Sing! Let your voices ring out!
A short little ditty or an hour long
As long as you are heard!
The sun sings with a tone that outshines all the others,
As he slides across the sky.
Before I can sing my own tune,
My breath is taken away
By the chirping of the stars,
The grass rustles out a hymn beneath my feet as I spin.
Just before the melody of my sleep
Joins the songs of others,
The harmony of the wolf and the moon
Lulls me into dreams of music.

Summar Khan

America Sings

America is always singing,
Singing songs of joy, hope, and freedom,
Songs adults hum on their way to work,
Songs that children sing with each other as they play happily,
Songs of a family on Thanksgiving when everyone is together.
Songs sung to cheer one up,
Songs of opportunity,
And lullabies our mothers sang us to sleep with.
Songs of pride and faith in our country.
America sings many different songs in many ways.
But the song that drowns out the others is the song that everyone knows in his heart,
America sings a song of love.

Miriam Levitin

Life's Song

A lighthouse sings ships' way home
Stars gleam and shine, singing reminders of the past, and promises for the future
The sun sings as it bestows light and warmth upon the earth
Rivers sing as they flow between banks, their bubbling sound adding to the chorus of song around them
A butterfly beats its delicate wings, sipping nectar from flowers in a soft but elegant song
A seed roots and slowly pushes itself up, singing as the tiny bud breaks the suface of the earth to face the sun
Rain falls to the ground, the fat drops hitting cold pavement in a rythmic song
A storm rages overhead, its song one of conflict eventually resolved
Waves crash on the shore, singing the song of the sounding sea
A beautiful song resounds as a human smiles; laughs; eyes lighting up with pure happiness
Eyes gaze, their song searching, reflecting the emotion behind them
A pulse beats, singing the sweet sound of precious life
Lungs breathe, their song the subtle sound of filling with and releasing air
Running is a song, sneakers slapping the ground in steady beat
Children play, their giggles a nostalgic song to old ears
A young child with its big eyes sings of curiosity and wonder
A person's courage and bravery sings of pride and honor
Love is a complex song, filled with joy and sorrow, carrying both memories and fate of the future
A dream is a fragile song of hope and promise
Life is full of exquisite, mellifluous songs; songs or remorse, songs of hope, songs of every kind possible imaginable
When you're lost, afraid, confused, hurt, lonely, inspired, curious, thoughtful, elusive, evasive, quiet yourself, be still the world. Just close your eyes, and listen. Listen to life's song.

Melvin Li

The Song of the Brooklyn Bridge

With the sun half an hour high in the west,
I enter the Promenade boardwalk basking in its golden rays.
I come from the east, the green fields way beyond Huntington Station,
To look at the storied bridge, the grand river, and the omnipresent seagulls.
Although a century and a half too late, I still want to listen to what Whitman had to tell the future generation he was anticipating.
And by crossing time's shores, catch the echoes of those songs he once sang
of America.

The Brooklyn Bridge! Its magnificent stone towers, facing each other across 1600 feet,
Soar into the sky, and its steel cables split the winds and sing of memory and time.
The stately and admirable river flows, its wave palling as the shores,
Singing of life, seasons, and eternity.
The seagulls still float in the sky, eyeing all and singing their untold stories,
And their bodies are painted a glowing yellow by the evening sun.
The bountiful hills of Brooklyn are beautiful as ever, full of humming and song,
But the tall masts hemming Manhattan have all vanished,
Replaced by a few speedy motorboats whose motors let out songs of power and
passion.

The Promenade boardwalk, hanging like a cradle of life over the six-lane traffic below,
Is filled with pedestrians of various kinds: men, women, young, old, where, black, and
brown...
All casually attired, approaching or passing, gazing or pointing, talking or laughing.
They look on the river and sky, their voices bubbly, excited, varying in cadence,
In all the flavors of English, some in unknown tongues.
Although I don't understand all their languages, I can hear hearts bursting into
songs of Whitman's democratic vistas.

Under the stone tower on the Manhattan side, a young man leans against the railings
And plucks at his guitar. I know not the tune, but my heart yearns to sing along .
I want to sing of the free spirit of America, soaring like the stone towers of the bridge
into the clouds.
I want to sing of the brave hearts of America, defending this land of plenty for all.
I want to sing of the omnifarious humanity on the bridge enjoying themselves on a
splendid day.
The Brooklyn Bridge! Of you I sing, a seasoned witness for the past 129 years of a
glorious city,
A quintessential landmark that bridges not only one brought to another,
But time's invisible shores so that my songs of America mingle with those of America's
greatest bard.

Melvin Li, First Place, Category E, Grade 11, Ward Melville High School, Mrs. Dilorio, 2012

Everything As It Should Be: Poetry Anthology

Cookie Crumbs

Fell into the armpit of my grandfather's chair
As I navigated an innocent world,
Where smoke stacks were cloud makers
And concrete protected worms.
My young mind turned what it couldn't understand
Into what it could bear to comprehend.
Even then deep within, I knew it was easier to pretend.
So that's what I did.
I quickly swept the evidence,
The crumbs rejected by my mouth,
In between the cushions before my mother could see.
The comfort of the chair swallowed me
and I fell asleep,
unconscious of the fact that one day
my world would crumble.
I slept for a long time.
I was six.

Grand Champions

2013

"Song of the Open Road"

Poet-in-Residence: Noami Shihab Nye

Philip Oreste

The Road to My Baseball Career

I hold my breath and wait for the ball to be caught.
Butterflies flutter around in my stomach.
The ball drops to the ground, I breathe out as I run.

I run in Babe Ruth's footsteps
Hitting just like him, home run after home run.
He is the baseball player I will be!

The road is long and hard
It is filled with mud, sweat and tears
I will meet its challenges.

It calls to me
I answer by doing my best
It is what I must do!

I will walk the green turf on the road toward my future
I will hope the sweet smell of victory will one day be mine.

This my path, This is my calling, This is my dream.
This Is My Road!!!

Hannah Lu

Song of the Open Road

The bold wide road stretches miles and miles across earth leading us to our dreams,
For I am a doctor knowledgeable and proper. I save many lives and make the world better.
For I am a teacher lively and happy. The future's destiny is in my hands to pepare the next generation.
For I am an architect brave and kind. My hammers play a lovely tune as I build houses for people.
For I am a mailman short and stout. I bring letters from loved ones and friends.
Reading them makes people feel so close to them.
Touchdown! I am a football player fast and fearless. I bring entertainment to the people and make their days happy.
For I am a librarian nice and informative. I give you access to my books to become smarter.
For I am a newspaper reporter exciting and energetic. I keep people in touch with the outside world.
For I am a marine biologist bright and a good swimmer. I save marine life so our animals will not be extinct some day.
For I serve in the army, faithful and self-less. I fight for my country's rights until we succeed and go home happily as winners.
For I am an artist creative and artistic as I smoothly swipe my paint brush smoothy against my paper, finishing the last stroke.
Do any of your dreams match any of the above? If yes, you must thank the open road.

Phaedra Damianos Conroy

The Rebirth of an Empty Mind

It's blank... It's blank!
There's no color, there's no thought.
This paper has no emotion, this canvas has no value.
I sit staring
Searching, yet finding nothing!

It bothers me, it frustrates me, my mind is ready to burst!
But it doesn't....
It's quiet, just this blank composition and I.

Then it begins again,
The torture once tamed is now overcoming me.
My heart is pounding, I'm trembling.
The walls are closing in! I can't take it anymore!

This manuscript mocks me, it provokes me.
I try to come up with something, but nothing occurs.
The emptiness is everlasting.

I lay back in my chair hopeless,
As if I were a mouse finally trapped in a corner by the cat,
Waiting for death! I hold my breath waiting
But noting happens...

I'm perfectly unscathed. I breathe out in relief.

No heavens have crashed upon me. I couldn't find a single scratch on my skin
Everything is fine... But I feel something.

I don't understand this bizarreness I'm feeling.
It doesn't throb, it doesn't sting, and it's not at all an agony or an ache.

It's beautiful, it's astonishing,
Like a sun set, it's color blending so elegant, or a cool sea breeze, freshening my face.

Then it comes to me, my mind is reborn.
The path to creation has opened.
Thoughts and ideas pour into my head.
Everything comes to ease.

I pick up my brush and all things known as creation cover the empty tablet.
Color, personality, dreams, and emotion are all shown in exquisite design.

After it's complete the result is thrilling.
Happiness and satisfaction find their way to my soul.

The emptiness inside had drifted away and now
I stand holding a master piece of greatness and perfection.

Phaedra Damianos Conroy, First Place, Category C, Mt. Sinai Middle School, Grade 8, Mr. Karl O'Leary, 2013

Courtney Taylor

Night Drive

On a journey through the night,
One sojourn finished, another new
There lies an empty span of road
An abyss of time, an unfinished song;
In the dark, our way is woven.

Lives flash and flicker in the background
Piercing the scene and roaring past
A crescendo in the middle of a half-written piece
Some lilts, some booms
Dragged off on odysseys of their own.

The night drives are hardly loved
In shadowed highways, only the distance is felt
And only the road is seen, the daunting expanse of life itself.

The song of the road lends itself to melancholy.
The gaseous scent and the loneliness
A traveling blur outside the cities and homes
But on the road, we are alive.

When the roads are empty, you can drive into the sky.
The song of the road is a song of sadness
But those who listen longest hear the underlying hymn.

Courtney Taylor, First Place, Category D, Massapequa High School, Grade 10, Mrs. Elyn Coyle, 2013

Kyle Fitzsimons

Untitled

The road I see is lined with trees
Then diverges into the open seas
I am on a road where I can travel all around
But first I must get through my academic life safe and sound
How will I choose to go about?
Well I haven't decided that exact route
All I know is one small principle
That I shall conquer my road and be invincible
I plan to prove my peers and superiors wrong
And show them my road is successful and strong
Like all roads mine will have a different obstacle or turn
But obstacles are meant to be a life lessons to learn
So far I have not let anything come in my way
To bring to where I am today
Far from whence I came
But my future will not be the same
I will travel through it with confidence and pride
And never let strength leave my side
The future is coming it's time to choose
The exact road that I decide to use
Get up, be there, be alert, be ready
Today I travel on this road steady

Jennifer Biancaniello

The Road Chosen for Me
from A Road of Many Directions: An Anthology

Life, a mysterious God of unequaled power
Whose fist clenches my throat and squeezes 'till I whimper.
Where is justice?...
I give in.
I have no power, no control, no right,
Continuation is the only road left to take.

Destiny is Life's forever best friend,
Hand-in-hand they bully me
Like a child in the playground.
Try, attempt to break their chains?
Impossible...
Why?

Everything has purpose.
All actions and decisions
Led me to a place unknown.
Life's will, Destiny's shove have broken me,
Transformed me,
Repaired me.

Perhaps I had no power... but everything is good.
Greatness, Happiness, Love may become my friends.
Thank you, Life.
Thank you, Destiny.
I started on your road unwillingly,
However, I stayed for myself.

Grand Champions

2014

"A Song of Joys"

Poet-in-Residence: Li-Young Lee

Violet Rand

"The Song of the Tap Shoes"

I see the building bright lights shining at me while I brilliantly tap dance.

Hear my tap shoes tapping acrros the floor. Tipitty-tap, tip-tap.

I feel the sweat pouring off me as I excitedly tap, shuffle-hop-step.

I tap dance to a jazzy song, "Working at the car wash, at the car wash, yeah!"

Fulap-step, fulap-step, shuffle-hop-step, shuffle-hop-step.

See the glittering blue costumes, the silver buckets and shammies.

See the bright faces with shimmering eye shadow and lipstick.

Hear the crowd wildly clap, and someone proudly say,

"It was like a song, tippitty-tap, tip-tap."

Kenny Silver

"Cat's Lullaby"

I hear it in a cat's purring.
A black cat curled up with its eyes closed, falling asleep.
From its chest comes a low rumble, a long, low continuous rumble.
The sound goes on for mere minutes before he falls asleep.
It seems like he is in a joyous mood.
If he wakes up, no purring at first, while he looks around, then slowly he starts to purr again.
A cat's lullaby to put himself back to sleep.

When I was young, just a baby,
my big black cat would come curl up next to me and sing his own cat lullaby that would set me to sleep.
Even though it was a rumbling, it was a very soothing song.
Whether he was intentionally trying to sing me to sleep, I will never know.

Behind the purring there is a rythmic beat, like the ocean's waves coming in and out.
The purr sounds like a soft breeze or a gentle patter of rain.
No matter how long two cats purr next to each other, they won't get in sync.
Each cat's purr is how own tune.

To me, a cat's lullaby is one of the most soothing sounds in the world and it make me very happy, no matter what mood I am in.

Ashley Luo

"Golden Melodies"

An intricate song,
Fabricated with the many sounds of delight,
Lyrics composed of gold,
Radiating to the waiting ears,
Around the world and across the oceans,
Like the bright sun,
Beaming in the light sky,
Spreading warmth to people everywhere,
Filling them with pleasure.
Melodies,
Songs trickle by,
Over green hills,
Down snow-capped mountainsides,
Weaving between branches,
In the sea of grean leaves.
Melodies,
Rising from clear water,
Flowing over smooth pebbles,
Spilling into the vast blue oceans,
Waves lapping in tempo,
Crashing against the jagged rocks of the day.
Melodies,
Emerging from brightly colored feathered throats,
Perched upon the trees,
Foilage rustling,
From the song of the breeze.
Melodies,
Jubilant notes riding on the wind,
Reverberating in the steep valleys,
Meandering to golden fields of wheat,
Swaying and dancing in unison,
To the joyful resonances.
Melodies,
Intertwined with the voices,
Of friends, family and neighbors,
To simply appreciate,
The gift of music,
Of the bliss it can bring,
Like opened presents on Christmas morning,
To young and old,
Rich and poor,
People of all ethnicities,
To rejoice together,
With the animals, plants and nature,
The golden melodies of joy.

Jocelyn Cheng

"Reasons"

For the newborn child
With small hands and a trusting grip

For the swells of a symphony
And the lights of a Broadway stage

For the triumphant slam of the door
Leaving the demon on the other side
And having the torture of sadness cease

For night skies filled with eternal light of silver stars
Broken solely by the arc of Apollo's chariot
As it leads on the venerated sun

For the glory of the game
The soft smack of leather against nylon net
For arms that rise triumphantly
For savage yawps and warrior cries

For all the seasons on the Earth
For crimson poppies and sun colored marigolds

For quenching the thirst for life
For feasting off of mountaintops
Or reaching the depths of the ocean

For knowing who you are
The colors that made you
The scraps of cloth, blood, sound, and feeling that made you
For being conscious of your skin

For seeing light
And light leave
Then realizing your mortality

For being valiant in fighting battles
That have yet to be won
For sherperding the blind
In that kind way of yours
Until equality is doled doubtlessly

For watching cracks in the concrete
As they drain substance from the last storm
Hear the gush of rain in the sewer pipes

And for realizing your are part of something infinitely bigger
That whose titanic magnitude you will never comprehend
For the simple pleasure of knowing
You have made it thus far
And it will go on
And there shall be more.

Tianru Wang

"Magnificient Day"

O, to capture the birdsong of the morning!
To hold with infinite satisfaction the darting piping thrill of hummingbirds
They - who nestle in the earthy sweetness of neroli on citrus trees rich with fruit,
Who praise the silhouette of branches against a dusk sky
And, ever faithfully, still to perfect the tableau

O, but to dwell eternally in the bright lights and bright laughter of an early evening!
The sun sourts the sea at seven o'clock, but the teachers, the reaerchers and writers trail home earlier, showering in the sparks of acheivement and scattering scintillas as they go.
The completion of day awakens relief, the progenitor of breathless joy.

O, the dreamer's joys!
Night, velvet and gentle, the fabric upon which dreams are embroidered-
I remember your peace. Beautiful as the deliberate pause of an orchestra-
the third beat before the solo of Vivaldi's Concerto in A minor-
enriching all that was before, and all that to be after.

O, to count the charms of the hours before dawn!
The city does not rest - the moon is mirrored behind kitchen windows,
planes cross stars overheard - yet primeval, pure solitude,
unilluminated with the light of day, glows in the darkness with the promise of silent miracles to come.

Tianru Wang, Category E, Santa Monica High School, CA, Grade 11, Chon Lee, 2014

Tatianna Spotorno

"Cello"

I run my tense fingers over the shining strings
Only I can hear the shy notes C G D A ringing quieter than a whisper
My right arm lifts the bow before I even think of it
I am prepared for what comes next

My hands move at the speed of this sound
This spirited song can almost play itself
The sweet music pours out from the cello- the extension of myself
I feel the deep vibrations with me- they travel from my head to my feet in an instant
I am only a witness to the sounds and feelings and emotions

Suddenly I feel free
What was once anxiety is now peace
There are numerous imperfections but the music created gives me joy, freedom, wisdom, a mythical emotion
I feel a strong sense of power, when in reality, I have none

As the music rolls along, my senses are focused solely on the little black notes
As though my life depended on it
The rest of the world is far from my mind when a song so intense touches the earth

The notes decelerate and my mind resurfaces as the overwhelming song draws to a close
The world is revived to its former state,
its bizarre condition before the provoking music happened
The song is complete but every beautiful note still floats through the quiet air
And echoes through my head.

Tatianna Spotorno, Category K, Mt. Sinai Middle School, Grade 8, Mr. Karl O'Leary, 2014

Crystal Huang

"Golden Concerto"
From A Song of Joy: An Anthology

A grand scheme of spotlights lit agianst the wooden stage blaring onto the entranced audience under the dimmed lights
Sound of the roaring waves under the moonlight, sound of birds flying to the third world
Trumpets blaring, strings of french horns against flutes, tiny pixies of piccolos surrounding the stage
Tiny silver and bronze angels floating, rising, reaching through the theater, across the air into the hearts of those fortunate for the taste of rhythm
Rhythm to the loud, domineering sounds of the thundering skies to the tranquility of obscurity of forests worldwide in the palm of my hands
The loud bass, the lonely oboes, the flightly flutes, the piccolos, the saxophone and alto saxophone, the clarinets, e-flat, b-flat, and e-flat alto-symphony of the heavens grounded by desire to spread its golden wings
Soprano Saxophone, Alto Saxophone, Tenor Saxophone, Baritone Saxophone playing all round, summer, spring, winter, and fall
The tuba, percussion, bells, drums, the lifting French horn - oh glorious, glorious indefinable beauty
An ethereal, heavenly ensemble transcendental forevermore

Rhapsody of heartbeats pumping simultaneously, rattling fingers, squeezed mouths, stomping feet,
Roving eyes from side to side to the nodding of heads in rhythm of the pounding, elavating, heightening-golden symphony
Lifting, soaring, ascending, controlling the innate conscious mind
Conscious of being induced to nothing, nothing but a puppet, a foolish entertained pet of music - yet alas, moving oneself is near, for time has played a petty trick on all those who were near
Time- a song that seeps through bones, bodies, hearts, swinging like a pendulum consistently
Diabolical, demonic, destructive to think otherwise

Sound of wings snapping in one fluid step, freeing and enveloping, embracing all within, devouring light and enticing life
Ba-bump Ba-bump, Ba-bump, Ba-bump, Ba-bump, Ba-bump, the echoing of thunder controlled and tamed under winter-skinned hands
Vivaciously, intrepid, unfettered-beating against the chains invisible to eyes
The unseen is proven to be seen, the skies cleared, sun showers, the moon hides, the clouds brighten, purple, apple scarlet, blues, yellows, orange and pinks

Grand Champions

2015

"Voice of the Elements"

Poet-in-Residence:
Yusef Komunyakaa

"Dear Mother Cloud"

Dear mother cloud, must I evaporate?

I fear I might never fall with the other droplets again.

And yet I dream; exploring the oceans and waterfalls of the world.

Swimming like a fish in the deep blue lake.

Flowing with the gushing water of the river.

And in the vast ocean, I shall fly with the crashing waves.

And then under the stifling sun

I disappear into an oblivion that no one knows.

I'll be back soon raining down drip drop drip drop

As I fall once again.

A lonely drop of water.

Colin Muessig

"The Elegant Earth"

I am the voice of the Earth, may these words be clearly heard and audible,

For I have a vital message to be delivered.

Such a marvelous planet should be treated like so, and its inhabitants must respect the requests of others.

My spirit has been present upon this land for all of eternity, and many sights, had I, the ability to savor.

I am the voice of the Earth, which may gradually fade away into nothing. May you answer my prayers, and set things just. Return nature to what it had once been.

Beautiful flowers, blooming in the gleaming sunlight, concealed my tall blades of grass, dancing in the spring breeze of a field.

Trees rooted within the soil, birds chirping in the treetops, and leaves rustling in abundance.

I am the voice of the Earth - diverse, nuturing, spacious, and vivid with every color imaginable.

Steep rocky canyons like a towering mountain, and deep grassy valleys digging down into the dirt.

I am the voice of the Earth - providing life and resources to all, maintaining beauty and serenity upon our planet.

Colin Muessig, Category B, Wisdom Lane Middle School, Grade 6, Mrs. Grubb/Mrs. Gallagher, 2015

Sarah Morgenthal

"I Run"

One last deep breath before I start the next chapter in my life.
I sprint ahead with passion, fueled by a fire that burns inside.

With earth below my every step and wind blown in my face.
I will not let it slow me down, I must finish this race.

I pull myself, step over step, ahead as land passes me to
New fields of view and new chances too, that I face as the time expires.

But I do not forget what fuels me, not water, not food nor pride.
A desire propels my every step that no element can subside.

A hunger to reach something to get to something more.
To carve a path out for myself one I didn't have before.

My destiny is calling, I must push myself ahead
To reach the points that I believe will eliminate regret.

I run each day, I run each week, I run each month, I run every year
Towards goals in life both near and far, bringing purpose to why I'm here.

This race is never ending in all the days I've known.
And if I win or if I lose, this race was on my own.

The life I lead, the path I take, this is my day in the sun.
My only day, my only life, before my flame burns out.

I run.

Isabelle Scott

"À Tes Souhaites"

(Sigh) gentle, the epitome of
Breath warm and wet with morning dew
Bestow a kiss of sunlight on the cheek of dawn
Like a string, bobbing and weaving
Through open windows, rippling curtains
Giggling
With good news.

(Sigh) tender, the essence of
Brush my lips with crisp reprieve
While the sun is beating as a pounding drum
A breeze through the trees is a flute
Which trills and leaves
(Just a whisper) of magic
By the sea.

(Sigh) peace, the embodiment of
Though some may argue the violence of the skies
Whipping and biting, thief of such trivials
As umbrella and life
I claim peace prevails in the mood and mind
Of prevailing winds, which know no time-
(For war or pain) They know only to blow, and blow again.

Eleni Aneziris

"The Spark of the Sun"

Upon overhearing articulations spoken by fiery blaze to reticent timber,
The forest fire, it proudly proclaims:
Hello King Tree, I am a socerer's promise, I am the mystic spark of the sun;
That orb in the sky lights me with its eyes, and I grace these hills come summertime,
In narrow puffs which breathe and behind the cautious wind,
In narrow slivers which reach up and throw caution to the wind,
I grow playful when meeting low-lying brush, dry twigs, fallen detritus;
From quiet ember I rise, a roaring inferno,
I crackle and curl, I am tall, I burn brilliant, I devour the fruits I am fed.

Had I been set by man, I'd engulf your outstretched dendrites,
And spiral into smoke clouds, leak past leaves into sky;
How I'd be ruthless, how I'd wreck acres, leaving fallow ground behind me,
The progressives, how they'd flood the place, crying oceans for humanity;
How I'd drag the miserable breath out of your wooden lungs, gasping,
How you'd be burnt and bare, standing there, quite alone, shivering,
Stunned into silence by my unforeseen fury, you'd crumble,
Into dust, blown across the graves of your beloved fellow brethren.

But I am nature-born; I respect my elders, when introduced to royalty,
My dear King Tree, I won't harm you;
I am but here to clear away dead foliage, lustful matches,
I can only edge around your damp, impenetrable barrier, and ignore those who are alive, inhaling,
I drink the oxygenn you provide, always licking my fingers of surplus air;
Do not despair when I leave without a shadow of warmth in my wake,
For departure allows the unearthing of fresh commencements,
And the ashes, they are celebrated profusely: the soil renewed, and enriched, for nativity.

Eleni Aneziris, Category B, Ward Melville High School, Grade 11, Lisa Rochford, 2015

Lindsay Stancampiano

"Alive"

I dance, unwillingly, around the battered brick fireplace that contains me;
how I long to escape this calamitous cage that confines me every night.
My actions are determined, not by myself, but by my merciless masters,
who watch me, intently, as I slowly die out, like a small child drifting of to sleep.
"Will I ever be free from this everlasting task of warming my masters on a chilly winter's day?"
I think to myself,
"Will I finally be able to explore a different part of this wonderful world that I have not yet seen myself?"

I am ignited, once again, and repeat the monotonous task I am assigned to perform.
I see my masters glide over to the hearth, their mesmerized faces slowly creeping closer to me,
focusing on the wisps of smoke that are emitted from my body.
The swirling smoke surrounds their surprised faces,
as distinctly I hear them start to gasp and cough up the thick smoke.
The event, while utterly unfortunate for my masters, seems to amuse me;
all I could think is that I wanted more...
                more...
                          more.

I feel ferocious flames spreading rapidly across my master's floor;
I hear their helpless cries piercing through the sounds of the crackling fire.
The smell of something burning is in the air,
and I feel a surge of power rush through every part of me,
reaching to the very edges of my body.
"I am finally free from the terrible cage of the fireplace, and my master!" I think to myself,
as a wide wicked smile stretches across my face.
I have never felt so alive.

Lindsay Stancampiano, Category K, Mt. Sinai Middle School, Grade 8, Karl O'Leary, 2015

Amani Hafeez

"The Age of Concordia"

An unimaginable world of harmony and peace,
Before might was right,
Before Earth was cruel.
When innocence was not ignorance,
When fear ceased to exist.
A world of peace, of love, of verity, of amity.
When Terra was the mother of all, and lover of all.
When the sun would rise through Elysian fields, people would
    dance and shout in joy to see their beloved Helios put on a
        show.
Not yet had human blood tainted Mother Earth and changed this
    paradise forever.
The needle of envy had not yet pierced the innocent thoughts.
Concordia, wandering here and there, would watch.
To see a world in ceaseless-joy which now habors avarice and
    greed,
To find hope, faith and harmony, then find greed, treason and lies.
The concept of Concordia, now locked in endless sleep,
Gone forever, disappeared and dissipated into the air.
In roots of trees you'll find it.
Concordia lost her silent battle. . . .
It seems it evanesced into particles unknown to man.
Blood of man has blemished to perfection of Elysium,
And though this world has lost all hope,
Maybe *you* will find some.
Open the jar Pandora left and find that Elpis stayed put.
If you open the jar,
And let her out of the confined space which has been her own for
    millenium.
Let the world know that Elpis is here.
And may they know that there is always hope for Elysium.

Amani Hafeez, Category L, JFK Middle School, Grade 6, Mrs. Rand/Miss Casey, 2015

Grand Champions

2016

"There Was A Child Went Forth"

Poet-in-Residence:
Robert Pinsky

Evelyn Soto

"Untitled"

The sun blazing into my cage of night whispering to me, wake up.

My head slowly lifts from my silky pillow.

A soul creeks into my thought's spirit.

The fire runs to my eyes like a burning ash.

The sun burning slightly like a dim light bulb about to go out.

My oak door creeks open

As my eyes leak open. *"Pop!"* The flower waking up after hibernation.

The smell of light licorice tiptoeing into my nose.

The cool breeze picking up to ignite the fire in my day.

My soul stepping onto the soft, silky grass.

The jagged day does not prevent the grass from linking with my heart.

The bumpy ride home is dim. When the water melts the fire, and the

Moon creeps out, my soul settles into the springing sunset of the

nightime shelter.

Marc David Nichitiu

"I Once Flew with Light"

I once went to the seashore to dance with the fresh salty breeze and to sing with pebbles. Splashing out in the waves, raising crowns of shiny droplets from the mirror of the sky, and it was raising sunny light rays everywhere around, gently touching my face and hands, I then looked up to the sky, and it rained more and more, with blue and yellow and white, and I danced with all its colors, which took me higher and higher, far from the green clamor. Up into the deep blue sky, up above the velvet puffy clouds, up beyond the aurora curtains, so I sailed through dust, to ride on a shiny swift comet, and to sing with the solar wind, closer to the Sun, to see its outbursts, to hear the powerful music of its vibrations, and then with a splash of energy, I surfed on the waves of our galaxy, swinging by its dark center, to slingshot out towards a quasar, far away, a whole galactic sun show, shrouded in mystery, to ride an incandescent slide towards two swirling black holes, dancing with each other, singing gravitational waves louder and louder, crowning shiny jets with splashing fiery colors; and their hands took mine and taught me how to feel the strings of dark matter, and how to see beyond the snowy screen of background microwave glow, into the winds of dark energy; so thus I became part of the spinning song played on the piano of the universe...

Gregory Kies

"Poet to Poet"

A child came forth bearing the name of Walter.
He came forth on May 31 from the world of the unknown and the nebulous,
To the world of being and life.
A child came forth in 1819 on the rolling, western green hills of Long Island.

A child came forth to the books and the world of literature.
A child came forth to the doctors and the lawyers, to ennui.

A child came forth to the classroom and to children,
To the wood-scented school and the old rickety stool.
A child came forth to a place full of sadness.

A child came forth to adulthood bearing the name of Walt.
A child came forth to the typesetters and to the journalists.
And to fame, for his work rose above him.

A child came forth to the horrors of war,
A child came forth to the air of soldiers.
A child came forth to show the needless suffering.

A child came forth, now an old man with a grizzled beard.
He came to the bookstores and to the schools,
To the poets, the men, and the women and the children.

On one sad day the old man again went forth,
He went to the world of the unknown and the lost on the 26th of March of 1892.
Many more children came forth after that day, bearing many other names.
But those children came forth to a world that was changed by writing,
By a child who came forth, bearing the name of Walter Whitman.

Gregory Kies, Catgory C, Plainview-Old Bethpage Middle School, Mr. Reinbold, 2016

"Paper is All Trees"

I was born in the year they thought the world would end,
When the people were selfish like wildfire they tell you not to feed.
They said they wanted a child before they died,
Even if their child died younger then they;
And that, was a game, an achievement to be made,
But when I was born, the world was smog and plastic.
As if we were meant to be surrounded by
The organized disaster of morning traffic, packaged lunch, and selfish nannies,
The sparkling-bluish-purple Hula Hoops, the Easy-Bake Ovens, the stuffed bunnies, giraffes, tigers and pandas,
The tiaras and trophies at the top of the shelf in the closet where no one can reach, the ice-skates leaning up against a wall of the garage in the hot summer next the dusty pink Schwinn.
Outside the grass rippled in all different directions like long hair, no intentions of impotence.
The wind blowing east at chimes on front porches
The red belly of humming birds whipping by like whirpools,
The lagoon brimming with mallards quacking for bread under gentle skies,
And seagulls, with greedy eyes, their black-tipped wings dripping like wet paint
There I patitently waited for the flesh and blood,
For the punchline when I would say my words, when the tired ends came to means.
That was the sallowness of where bones begin and counterfeit ends,
But the smiles were marginal and
My eyes were tempted to blink.
There were times when I forgot my existence;
I saw myself on stage with the painted faces, nude tights, and character shoes,
The exaggerated expressions, the costumes that conceal actors that manipulate the minds.
They kept the stage cold so the nervous heat didn't win,
But on the stage I was not nervous;
I was only cold,
So I forgot
Life beyond performance,
The melting pot of flowers on the face of the hills, the rabbit dug railways underneath the ground,
the soaked green cypress saplings, the banana slug kisses, the barked aspen with blonde leaves, and
the sun setting, lowering toward the grasses, threatening to set them on fire.
I forgot, that I too,
Am paper, once made from trees
I think
Sometimes that I see myself, growing beneath a canopy of branches
Their limbs stealing the sunlight,
And beneath the canopy, I reach past the height of the limbs around me
Until I have room to
Catch fire of the rising sun

Nathalie Esther Amazan

"Intertwined Cosmos"

I am not only a moment,
I am all the moments that were, that are, and will be,
I transcend these three to somewhere...
something of a beautiful and spiritual dimension we all know.
The way the bitternut hickory greens as it signs in the beginning of the March season, brings me
its peace;
and as the ocean rises and falls, my soul moves along with her, because we have known each
other before I was born.
Each ascending sunrise followed by the descending sunset, with distinct, coalesced shades;
The insects that bring life to these plants,
These plants that bring life to me;
Beautiful cycle of humanity, this is the constitution of my anatomy.
The motion of these waves I stand before, are the reason for my heartbeat,
The gentle air hugging my body whispers oxygen to my lungs, and I listen to this oxygen move
swiflty down the path they've made, and I think:
"How beautifully elegant."
Thoreau has become a part of me:
"Simplicity, simplicity, simplicity," these simple things are of me.
The laughter of my mother,
Ambition of my father,
The awe-filled defiant natures of my brother and sister,
Each are inscribed on the neurons transmitted throughout my body,
They come to make their home and color my DNA.
The reflection I see of myself
Shows Saturn's rings circulating this body of mine in all of its glory,
Pluto's newfound majesty in my own eyes,
And stardust exhaling like a cloud from my breath.
I am Water that keeps me alive,
I am Fire that burns deep,
I am Earth that reminds me of my composition,
I am Air I inhale,
I all moments, I am.

Amani Hafeez

"Child of Wisdom"

There once was a child that leaped from the head of Sapientia.
Precocious as a baby bird, she left her little nest in search of
   answers to her endless questions.
She found earth all by herself, without the help of any goddess
   or man.
She thirsted for knowledge, and went out to find it.
She saw scholars immersed in books, their minds brimming
   with intelligence.
Their minds became her mind, clever, yet lacking balance.

She observed elderly smiles, showing their wits and their scars.
Their smiles became her smile, radiant and true.

She witnessed skilled workers, able to cure and heal with her gentle hands.
Their hands became her hands, learned and calloused.

She watched as the scientist exhumed solutions from his heart.
His heart became her heart, beating as a clock ticked.

She glimpsed venerable souls, knowingly waitng for the clock to tick, and never
once looking down at the strap on their wrist.
Their wrists became her wrists, worn with time.

She espied wizened wizards, peering at sparks of memory.
Their sparks became her spark, fueling her studies and perceptions.

The child of Sapientia, searching far and wide, found light in the eyes of the
human beings, fire in the hearts of the engineer.

She renewed the world, revolutionary and new.

Amani Hafeez, Category F, JFK Middle School, Grade 7, Mrs. Friedman, 2016

Lizette Kelly

"My Seasons"

I go forth every day.
Seeing objects that become my day.
As I go forth I see the real meaning of the objects.
And in the day the objects shall become me.
The objects of summer shall become me.
The feeling of the warm sand is like the sun, sending warmth througout me.
The scatter of koi searching for food is like fireworks on the fourth of July covering the sky, shall become me.
The objects of winter shall also become me.
The excitement of the horses seeing their first snowflake is like watching a baby with a new toy.
And the geese getting ready to fly south for winter,
Which is like how my family is flustered getting ready for a vacation, shall become me.
The objects of fall shall become me too.
The rows of bright orange pumpkins waiting for picking remind me of jack o'lantern contest my brother would have.
The taste of candy apple reminds me of the ones that my family get for the celebration of Christmas, shall become me.
And the objects of spring shall become me.
The lily pads holding the frogs are like a helping hand showing care.
The croaks of frogs breaking the calmness of the day, making me realize that I should come to the pond.
And the beautiful purple, red and orange colors of the sunset are like a field of flowers that I run through, shall become me.

Grand Champions

2017

"Dreams"

Poet-in-Residence:
Marilyn Hacker

Tessa Burke

"A Beautiful Song, A Beautiful Sound"

A beautiful song, a beautiful sound, it feels like I'm in a dream

I hear a song, a beautiful sound, upbeat it is I hear

It can be soft, it can be loud

It is sittin' in the sand, right next to a cactus

I pick it up and start strumming along to the beautiful upbeat song

A beautiful song, a beautiful sound, it feels like I'm in a dream

I hear a sound, a beautiful song, it will lead me to my destiny

I put it back right next to the cactus sittin' in the sand
I slowly walk away

A beautiful song, a beautiful sound, it feels like I'm in a dream

A beautiful song, beautiful sound

I see a little girl, staring at the guitar

She looks at me and I look at her

She picks up the guitar and smiles and starts strumming along to the beautiful upbeat song

A beautiful song, a beautiful sound,

That's what I hear.

Muskan Kumar

"I Dreamed a Dream of a Brand-New World"

I dreamed a dream in the quiet stillness.
Echoes of silence filled the dark, starry night sky.
My dream spoke to me,
I knew that she wished me no harm,

My dream gives me delight, happiness, and she gives me cheer,
She transports me to a world where war isn't spoken of or seen,
A place where peace and pleasure join hands,
A world where Christians, Jews, Buddhists, and Hindus live in harmony,
They all sing hymns together,
Their songs are elegant and free,

No fights, no worries, no fear,
A pleasing place where anyone can be anything, and do anything,

My dream embeds a good mood within me,
She makes me smile.
I feel jubilant, phenomenal and free,
I am in a wonderful world,
A great place to be,

I dreamed a dream on a dark, starry night,
I dreamed a dream with no fear, only peace and happiness,
A dream where the smiling faces of children light up the day as they run and play,

My dream speaks to me,
She declares this to be a blissful place,
A peaceful place, a place without worry,
A prodigious place to live, to be free, and not be judged for who you are,
A world with helpful people,
A world where all want to live,

I dreamed a dream in the quiet stillness.
Echoes of silence filled the dark, starry night sky,
My dream spoke to me.

Muskan Kumar, Category B, Wisdom Lane Middle School, Grade 6, Mrs. Grubb, 2017

Nathan Barry

"The City That was Mine"

I dreamed that love was in the air between the people of a certain city,

A city of harmonious people who helped each other up and shared.

They were kind, and it was if they were one.

Every voice spun through the air and was caught like a ball,

Every opinion was voiced, and the city advanced in compromise and joy.

A beautiful harmony, majestic and graceful like a bluebird,

And the buzz of the town's people flew,

While sounds of chit-chatter rang like a bell.

The sweet soothing serenading smell of Grandma Sally's pie,

Wafted and danced in the streets,

A melody that kept the land they lived in alive. But most of all,

They listened, they heard, and they understood

When they grew more, and understood more.

It mattered not the land of their birth, or the shades of their skin.

Strength comes in numbers, while numbers come from uniting every voice,

The voice of agreement and disagreements taught about their life and beliefs.

It was happy and the passion of the people was a red rose on every windowsill

In that dream of a city that was mine.

Hadar Leybov

"Disaster"

I dreamed a dream; the future is a disaster and full of violence,
Parents and children trying to run away from what the future has in store for them
Technology advanced to such an extent that it dominates the world, provoking a war between the past, present, and the future.
A world of prosperity became a world of survival.
This all began when humans created inventions enabling them to become lazy and dependent.
People started to forget what a beautiful world we have,
And the memories started to fade away.
They stayed inside, focusing on technology, a distraction from reality.
This led people to creat machinery that did all the missions and taks for them.
People didn't have to leave their comfort zone to attend work; they had a three-dimensional holograph representing them, as if they were there.
Electricity held the world together like glue holds shreds of paper.
Unfortunately, the electricity had too much to handle and it erupted:
A worldwide pandemic occurred. Memories of the past came and spread throughout the world like shooting star flying through the atmosphere.
People realized that the life before this millennium was peaceful and joyful, unlike the violence and disaster they had in the future.
Parents took their children to parks, swung their kids on swings, took them to beaches, the color so blue ... they played in the sand, building volcanoes and sand castles.
In the future, children didn't have the experience like the children from the past had. Their entertainment was technology.
They played video games, their life was coverd with screens and light, like a baby covered with a blanket.
Adolescents didn't go to school; school went to them. The education they recieved was the teachings of technology.
Technology is a very helpful tool. But too much of it can lead to things beyond our reach.
Although the past is the past; we can still apply the past to our present and future.

Sophia Takvorian

"Tall Grass"

Somewhere in this grand shade,
I find you, asleep, dreaming
of far different things than me,
yet you're shining
so fervently,
floating,
that it only makes sense
that we'd be dreaming of the same thing.
I, expressly with that glow
you marked me with,
and you, you otherworldly thing,
with that radiance
and mysticism
of a luz opal,
a galaxy within you,
projected without.

And I dream;
O, what have I done to deserve you,
you being rapture, of reverie?
And I think
what have I done to myself,
so entranced by a single enigma
of breathless melancholy?
Whose song should I sing but mine?
Wrapped in your wonder,
drowned in your shade,
I crawl, I crawl, I crawl.
and I know
unloving hurts more,
and I'm so green for loving you;
all tall grass and innocence.

But I open my eyes,
just as the light finds its way through our window,
its rays sleeping silently next to you,
and curving with the corner of the room.
I dreamt you were hovering over me,
not letting any light through,
a soft whir sounding around us.
But as I watch your chest expand and collapse,
the way the light bends with the lines in your face,
your softness overpowers you.
Our dreams are fragmented around us,
pieces blending with all things under the sun,
both confessed anf unfamiliar.
My solitary dream was no divination;
no shade's that big in this radiant world.

Sophia Takvorian, Category E, Manhasset High School, Grade 12, Mrs. Kannengieser, 2017

"Who Am I??"

I am the body of darkness you fear,
I am the pleasure at night you crave,
I am what leers near,
I am the night you were depraved of,
I am the cousin of death,
The image of everything you're infatuated with,
I am what makes people,
Breaks people,
I am your worst nightmare and best friend,
I am you,

I woke up last night and figured I would try to figure out what it means,
To be dreaming of falling for a reality that's better than yours,
One where we don't live, walk, talk, and breathe nightmares,
Instead we live, walk, talk and breathe the change we wanna be,
And one where we use the information we have properly,
I don't know what scares me more,
The fact that close to half of America has some sort of mental disorder,
Or the fact that we still don't help them,
And I don't know what's more appalling,
The fact that 23.5 million Americans suffer from addiction,
Or through the mist of thier affliction only 11% of them will get to end the suffering,
Or maybe the worst thing yet that we qualify addiction as a chronic disease,
But we'll throw addicts in jail with ease,
If we crunch some numbers we can see that's 1 in 10 Americans,
That's 10% of your population rendered useless and the only thing you can do is pass more laws that's viewed as abusive?

I am the body of darkness you fear,
I am the pleasure at night you crave,
I am what leers near,
I am the night you were depraved of,
I am the cousin of death,
The image of everything you're infatuated with,
I am what makes people,
Breaks people,
I am your worst nightmare and best friend,
I am you,

While my dreams may be bright and peaceful,
I'm still rather dark and cynical,
No, I'm still rather dark minuscule,
But the dream of making it better today is what drives me at the end of the day cause out the concrete this rose came.

Grand Champions

2018

"Tribute"

Poet-in-Residence:
Vijay Seshadri

Bailey Brett

Ode to the Night

Night murmurs
Night darkens
Night slowly tumbles in.
Night dips into the cool sky.

Night flows
Night swerves
Night slips through my window,
dims my cozy room.
Night soothingly sings a lullaby
to all.

Night mingles
Night mutters
Night glides into town
Night covers the world
in a blackened tarp.

Night sails
Night soars
Night soothes deeply in our
hearts and then night
takes over and
all is black.

Boone Davis

Times Square

I see people emerging from
the tunnels that pierce through the
guts of the stone giant
that we live and
depend on.

I see metal boxes taking
turns gliding through the streets,
making loud noises of
irritation every few moments.

I see flashing lights, boasting
images of everything imaginable,
but nobody falls for their
tricks; they know them too well.

I see travelers marveling over
this strange context,
which makes them seem
out of position of people
passing by.

I see everything acting the
Way it always does; playing its
Assigned role, improving
A balance,
Throughout the busy day.

Adriana Pioli

My Mom

If I am beautiful, it's because I look like you.
If I am strong, it's because you showed me
      that I can do anything I set out to do.
If I make a mistake, it's because you showed me
      how to pick myself up and move on and learn from it.
If I am kind to strangers, it's because you showed me
      the meaning of compassion.

If I am a good friend, it's because you taught me
      to treat people the way I'd like to be treated.
If I am a good Christian, it's because you taught me.
      to pray when I'm at a loss and need help.
If I am wise, it's because you taught me
      if I don't have anything nice to say, don't say it all.

When life wasn't always good to you,
      you always made it positive.
You are the strongest woman I know.
I am thankful for your wisdom, advice,
      and your words of encouragement.
I am thankful for everything you are
      and everything I aspire to be.
I am most thankful that I can proudly call you
      my mom.

Adriana Pioli, Category C, Grade 8, Grand Avenue Middle School, Ms. Silvestri, 2018

Kara Kokolakis

The Place of Laughter and Tears

The theatre is like a home -
Happiness and strife all around you.
It's a place of laughter and tears.

The smell of glue and paint on the set of the stage
Hits you as soon as you walk through the big double-doors,
And the freshly-inked programs overpower any other scent in the room.

You find your seat,
Pushing past the tightly-grouped people
Who are chattering and chattering away.

The show starts, the lights dim, and suddenly the audience is near silent.
The talented performers work their magic,
And you can tell they love what they do.

You can hear the young girl in seat L16 singing along with every song.
Her mother is shushing her, but she doesn't listen.

Or maybe you're the one on the stage,
Trying not to pay attention to the girl in seat L16.
You stifle a chuckle, as you were once just like her.

You know your lines, you know your blocking.
The choreography you know all too well.
But you're still fearful
Because you may forget to giggle on page 5
That was added an hour before opening.

This is all you've been waiting for.
Either you're watching, or you're on stage.
You can't hide the excitement you feel
Because you're here
In the place of laughter and tears.

Kara Kokolakis, Category C, Grade 8, Mount Sinai Middle School, Mrs. Wallace, 2018

Katriel Murphy

The Police Officer

To the police officer who found me
An abandoned helpless infant in a basket
So close to death that I could have been in a casket
On the foggy empty dark morning streets
You saved my life by giving me a chance
And now instead of begging for food, I get tucked into my sheets

To the police officer who found me
In so little time I was taken into an amazing family
One that can provide what the other could not
They have surrounded me with love and support every child wishes for
Because of you, my life is filled
with extraordinary experiences and outstanding oppurtunities

To the police officer who found me
Thank you

Katie Gozaloff

Respect the Badge

As we near the twenty-first hour of the day
And my fatigued body winds down from the busy day
My dad kisses me briefly on both cheeks and says goodbye
For I won't see him till the morning
When the sun rises and the sky is colored orange and yellow
'Till he is done with his midnight shift
All through the night he fights crime as flashing lights shine red and blue,
Speeding down the poorly-lit street, hurrying to yet another call,
In the middle of the night it gets hard to resist your eyes shutting,
Indeed it's always a long night, but he still has a job to do.
Being part of the police department can be difficult and dangerous,
So through the night I pray in my dreams for his safety
And continue my hopes through my very deep slumber
Until I wake up with another kiss and a soft touch from his frosted hands.
I know now he is safe after a quite eventful and wintry night
And the joy of seeing his face and red cheeks,
It is yet another day that I'm so extremely thankful for him and others
For all the grueling and tough nights.
They should be highly respected and not just by some
But by all for risking themselves to serve and protect the community.

Katie Gozaloff, Category D, Grade 9, Sayville High School, Mrs. Tisha Anne Werner, 2018

Sarah Lewis

Flight Feather

I soothe myself amongst the lines
which warble from beneath my pen,
which flutter in their heedless pace,
which scratch across the paper's skin.
A bath of words to soothe the ache,
a balm of words to heal the scratch,
words to pump within my veins,
a flock of thoughts for words to catch.
Bold and black, dark, distinct,
my thoughts are not confined to ink,
but soar along on papered wings,
and my heart with them;
the paper sings.

Daniella Graffeo

Praise for the Past

Sunset Beach

I stood at the shore of the ocean last night,
The sky a fiery canvas painted with lemon yellows, blazing oranges, and flamingo-feather pinks.
Waves crashed the shore hard, then soflty, as if the ocean was attempting to tell me a message.
Out of nowhere, the tides delivered a green glass bottle at my feet.
Not knowing where it came from or where else it had been, I found a message curled inside.
I pulled out the cork and dropped the scroll into my hands, it being drenched from some secret
saltwater that slipped inside, seeping into the secrets of the sea.
I could barely make out the words, but I only found three:

Look around you.

And the letter disintegrated through my fingers, back into the sea.

Granting the letter's wish, my eyes scanned the beach and found wonders all around me.
The grainy sand making a home between my toes.
The ocean and the land trading shells through the waves; in and out.
Seagull silhouettes dark against the flaming colors of the sky.
The sun slowly slipping into depths of the sea.
The wind blowing through my thick, wavy, dark hair, touched with a hint of salt.
A huge sandcastle, standing just for a family of snails or crabs.
Scattered tide pools, filled with baby starfish and urchins hugging the sandy walls for protection.
The clouds providing beds for the incoming stars to rise and dance on, illuminating the night with their light.

When you get the chance, look around at the wonderful world around you.
You'll never know what you might see or miss in life until you open your eyes.

Grand Champions

2019

"To Realize the Future"

Poet-in-Residence:
Jane Hirshfield

Lia Rewkowski

The Evolution

The evolution will always be coming like the warm glow of the everlasting light on a freezing day.

Carrying us into high skies!

Seeing how high even the fierecest winds will take us!

The evolution of mankind, leaving history in the past and leaping into the future!

Seconds, minutes, decades, centuries!

The future will not stop coming no matter how long it takes.

The changes are coming, fast or slow they will still be coming.

They will always be coming like the everlasting light on a cold, freezing, windy day.

Cristian Martinez

A Glimpse of Tomorrow

We have torn down walls before
I dream of a future without any hate and war
No caskets being flown home
Where family members are left to mourn
Instead, I see a beautiful cascade of colors
Children living with no fear
Families not being ripped apart
Just for not being born here
No need for police and soldiers to barge into homes
Checking identities, judging and telling a family they must go
A world with no hate is what I see
I will tear down the walls with words I choose to speak
We must unite, start to fight
It all starts with one person's courage
Go ahead and build your wall
We will tear it down, just as we have before

Kate Sun

Thank You, Nest

As laugh lines sink into my skin,
I travel alone into lonelier woods.
My mother's watchful eye grows distant, and I peer forwards, mind unshackled.
Whistles of independance haze and leer,
Filling the air with dust -
Lungs suffocating, eyes stinging,
But when the wind settles,
My abrasions no longer throb.
Laugh lines shrink deeper,
Yet my hands claw, even more voraciously,
For bracnches unseen, but desired.

Ryan Derasse

Technology Is Taking Our Lives Away

In 2050 technology is taking our lives away and is melting our brain.
thirty years ago the old joke of momma screaming johnny you're gonna end up on the
streets when you get older because of your electronic addiction
and johnny laughing because he thinks that momma is just trying to scare him
well that johnny is me. I should have listened.

I was strolling along the street with my fancy phone and I saw a less fortunate family
who didn't have enough money to get into a park.
instead of being upset they acted like they were in a party that was worth a fortune.
they had a barbeque and they were laughing and playing as if nothing was wrong.
I didn't see one phone or computer, which shocked me.
but maybe what I was really thinking was how fortunate they were to not be ruled by
electronics.

I continued on my walk checking my phone from time to time when I saw a family
that spent extra money on a cabana and I didn't see any eye contact at all.
they didn't even attempt to socialize with each other.
all they did was play on their phones not appreciating what they had.
it sickened me. I took a note on my phone.

then I saw a family who were using their phones for a game.
it was weird because they were having so much fun with a game on the phone.
all of a sudden the phone died.
the family was in shock and the fun died too.
the parents blamed each other as the kids screamed and cried
it was a disaster. I checked my phone battery to make sure that doesn't happen to me.

next I saw a family near them with the exact game just not on the phone.
the kids were laughing and yelling to help dad get the word and mom was trying to go
into some funky poses to help dad too.

it is the future. please spread the word technology doesn't create happiness.
today was the day I realized we need to change so we can become our best selves.
we need to use tachnology less.
what do you think?

Greta Flanagan

Words

Words! Words! Words!
The ability to control and create with only pen and ink!
To bring someone to life with simple black strokes,
And to fill them with emotions as clear as day -
Images and people float off paper with clarity and feeling,
And fly, like a black raven soaring across our thoughts,
They are honored, in one mind, in two, in a thousand -
What a wonderful ability, to create such a thing,
How joyous it would be, to connect future millions with only prints,
How joyous, indeed, if that were me.

Greta Flanagan, Category D, Grade 10, Oyster Bay High School, Ms.Murphy, 2019

The Cost

I hang my head in shame,
Fearful to look up and observe the world around me,
Bustling with industry and production, which eat away at the Earth,
Choking her, stripping away at her resources, setting her land and oceans aflame,
She does not resist, for all she can do is watch,
As the air takes each puff of pollution like a punishment,
And species flee north, endangerment, extinction on their tails,
And the ice caps cry countless tears, joining the ocean, whose levels rise in defeat.
This is her fate, sealed by humanity.

Progress is the governor of the future,
He soothes humanity's guilt,
Claiming that we must pillage the Earth to satisfy our pursuit of advancement,
The exploration of sciences, delving further into genetics, space, psyche,
The refinery of technologies, becoming swifter, sharper, sleeker, superior,
The shift from humble wood houses, to lavish stone castles, to sleek glass constructions,
Boundless buildings which stretch their slender metal palms to the sky,
Begging to reach further, breaking new boundaries, pushing conceived limitations
until there is nothing in their way,
They pave a path for Imagination, who joins Progress hand in hand,
Guiding us to the future, at the Earth's expense.

For all its glory, advancement cannot mask corruption
Poverty still flashes his face in the streets, sporting the most wicked of grins,
His sister, Gluttony, beams with pride as she watches us succumb to her calls,
While Rage storms the Earth's terrain, provoking indecency, Violence, and war,
Atop a throne, Greed watches, cold, calculating,
Persuading us to renounce mortality when there is money to be made

I pray that future generations will overcome these challenges,
Reviving the Earth before she takes her final breath,
Pursuing innovation without becoming blinded by hatred and material gain,
Recreating a future of advancement, without the cost.

Tiffany Jiao

Sweet Poison

America…the beautiful?
Through screens, a parasite spreads a deadly electric plague.
It reflects a mesmerizing metallic color, sweet poison to my eyes.
Blinding white light of the digital world enchants and entices me;
I fall under its dark spell and become madly addicted to its keen, but baleful, sting.

America…the beautiful?
No longer can I recall the sound of crackling leaves as they dance during the midst of autumn.
No longer can I recall the way the golden rays of sunlight fragment off waves of the salty sea.
No longer can I recall the subtle intertwinement between the violet clouds and azure swirls of summer skies;
I lie under the coral sunrise in a field of fresh daisies, only to find myself looking down at the screen in my hands, hypnotized by the sweet poison of white light that reflects into my eyes.

America..the beautiful?
How can I be aware of this America if I allow myself to be blinded?
How can I be aware of this America if I do not cure myself of this addiction,
this illness of the mind?
How can I be aware of this America if I allow my heart to be torn out,
and watch as it is replaced with cold pieces of animatronic gears?

America…. the beautiful.
I finally open my eyes to the vast wonders around me.
I free my soul from technology's deadly grasp.
I finally realize that sight is a gift, and that I had been chipped.

I see
the land of the free, and the home of the brave.
I see
the beautiful bouquet of diversity filled with a vast array of colors and shapes.
I see
the power that human connection and love holds over violence and chaos.
I see
the true America that exists behind the screen stitched to the skin of my palm.

Daniella Graffeo

"The Utopian Dystopia" from *The Utopian Dystopia*

One day, in the future,
Hundreds, maybe even thousands of years from now,
The world will be a much different place.
Mankind will spend centuries improving technology,
Only changing the world to improve human lives,
Not caring about all of nature's features cowering behind massive buildings
Or being crushed by newfangled cars.
Mortals would think they have it all,
Living each day like the last,
Rising with the wakening sun,
Scuffling down golden streets all day,
Then collapsing in bed when the sky puts on its deep blue nightgown.
But what if the very next day, the sun didn't rise?
Then what would humans do?
Would they wake up and just sit in bed, anxious to see a familiar morning light?
Would they even wake up at all?
How would people get around, if the sun never rose again?
They wouldn't be able to see the intense "utopia" that took so many years to build around them,
And the world would be pitch black.
The only way to see the future would be to resort back to the past,
By using oil lanterns or miniscule flickers of light.
And in those little fires people will see the gold roads they once walked on turn coppery.
On the mighty city's outskirts, they would find bruised flowers,
Drained of color and resting for an eternal nap.
They would find burnt stumps of once enormous trees,
The only thing left of those trees the rings of their age,
Showing how long they have lived before their tragic deaths.
They would find wide-stretching ditches where lakes used to be,
The water gone, already evaporated,
Attempting to vanish in the air like ghosts to escape human grasp.

And maybe, just maybe, that day will be branded in people's minds,
As they shuffle around in the dark,
The day when they all realize that taking advantage of the world around them
Never should have been a desired plan.

Matteo Spotorno

If Only the Planet Had Been Saved

Earth steadily grew smaller in the distance.
People looked out into space, watching it disappear.
The planet was not to be visited again.
It was free of humans at last.
Ships were headed away from this place.
People wished that they could have stayed.
If only the planet had been saved.
Earth's demise had been building for a while.
Autumn and Winter grew shorter and warmer.
Summer grew longer and took over.
Storms grew stronger and stretched larger.
Glaciers grew smaller and melted until they were gone.
Coastlines grew further inland and encompassed cities.
Cities grew overcrowded and polluted.
Grass grew less green and healthy.
Animals grew weaker and rarer with time.
Poor grew further into poverty and starvation.
Wealthy grew more powerful and power hungry.
Governments grew corrupt and careless.
War grew more frequent and intense.
Disease grew widespread and rabid.
Faith stopped growing.
If only the planet had been saved.
People wished that they could have stayed.
Ships were headed to a better place.
A new planet would be host to humans.
It would be their second chance.
People looked into space, planning their new lives.
Earth disappeared in the distance.

Grand Champions

2020

"The ship is clear at last, she leaps!"

Poet-in-Residence:
Juan Felipe Herrera

Noor Alzafarani

"Great Wonders of the Sea"

Leap year every four years,
    It is one of those years,
        Oh great wonders of the sea, I leap for you!

A bright sunlit zone of glistening and shiny water,
    Carefully a shelled turtle swims,
        A school of freely exotic, colorful fish passes.

Lower to the next layer, the twilight zone,
    A very vicious, deadly, so scary migrating massive shark.
        A bold, baby crab swimming closer,
            The crab's activity is astonishing, as it burrows in the sandy sea bottom,
            Such an amazing sight to see!

Further down the dark blue sea,
    A stunning starfish,
        Harmless looking,
            But for one eye on the tippy tip of each tapered and pointed arm,
            I touch the starfish; it is rough, fuzzy, frizzy and so spiky.

Down deeper, a perfect peace,
    I hear bubbles, big and bouncy,
        Or so I thought.

Pollution, such pollution!
    A threat that will savage and damage our world!

Corals should be colorful and as hard as rock,
    Here, these sea corals are smooth, spongy, lacking luster, colorless.
        Seals, dolphins, and fish trapped and tangled in the unnatural, too.
        Sea life dying unnaturally.

I see all this with my eyes,
    Like a soaring eagle sees the sea while flying high.
        I come out of the sea, an outstanding breeze.

Oh great wonders of the sea, I leap for you!
    I promise myself to explore and examine more of earth's glories and grandness!

Noor Azafarani, Category A, Gracdes 3-4, Southwest Elementary School, Ms. Robin Kerns, 2020

Izyaan Burney

"Changing the World"

I want to leap into a world where there is peace
Where no one is judging you by your race, religion, and identity

I want to leap into a world where people care about the planet
And realize that we only have one home

I want to leap into a world where people respect each other
And know that people are created equal

I want to leap into a world where there is no conflict on power
To keep countries in peace and not war

I want to leap into a world where there is no violence
Where we could only use words to express ourselves

I want to leap into a world where children have the right to learn,
To access more knowledge, to build future

I want to leap into a world where people can make a difference
A difference to change the world

I want to leap into a world where people have a home
To help the struggles of homeless people around the world

I want to leap into a world where people can make a difference
A difference to change the world

Ray Zhang

"Japan"

We arrived at Narita Airport
and rode a fast train into the Japanese countryside
past the rice fields,
rows of grass that look like football fields,
a satisfying shade of green,
past manufacturing plants and towns,
past telephone poles,
arriving at a modern, yet traditional city-
bright candy-colored lights
like a kid's best friend.
The night market welcomes
so many people I could get lost.
We drank green matcha tea
in a colorful little tea shop,
we saw the open air Picasso Museum
on top of a mountain,
and a Buddhist temple hidden in the trees.
Mom took pictures, standing back 50 yards,
and rushing to keep up.
Together we leaped into
our time together
before Brother goes back to college,
Father goes back to work,
and I go back to school.

Ray Zhang, Category C, Grades 7-8, Windemere ranch Middle School, Ms. Sheri Herauf, 2020

"Counting"

Don't count your mistakes
there aren't enough
numbers for all of us

I think I must have stolen
almost all of them
many summers ago
one by one
in my open hand

when waves didn't ripple
but crashed inside mixing
the unblemished grains of sand
with my broken guilty shells

When you put your ear to listen
the crying song of the ocean was
from me
but You, You

            leapt
                        into the stormiest of waves

and sang with me

because we can't save ourselves
but we can save another

Now I place my hands
over your lips
and beg
you to stop counting
please

Let us all bound across the tide
and find our shore

"Old White Skates"

You put on your old white skates
full of scratches, unsharpened blades,
too tight like undersized sneakers
and the rink smells like blade-cut rubber mats
with a hint of soggy wood.
Stepping from friction to frictionless,
you feel the familiar glide,
hear the sounds of blades scraping.
Past you, kids skate like bullets-
red cheeked, sniffly noses, gloves with holes.
Coaches yell, Watch out!
You try to watch out-
back then, words were noises like waves,
you didn't need to listen.
Now didn't as the westfit of aging as you spin
though you're only seventeen.
You're not in your own body,
you're not an adult, not the person going off to college in a year.
Now, you're just a kid on the ice,
ten years old again.
You remember your old self, not chained by the tugs of gravity
or the lack of second chances
but free like a kid on the monkey bars, on the seesaw, on a slide,
like a kid with Barbie Doll curtains, bubblegum toothpaste, and white-out nail polish,
like a kid who falls without bruises.
When you put on your skates,
your blade retraces your travels, your turns, and your stops.
You remember that you will never forget
the dreams of the girl with the old white skates.

Shriya Vaddigiri

"Some People" from "Journey Through Reality" Anthology

      Every year, we go outside, who knows how many times?
  In the Spring, people plant bright blooming flowers, which take in their beloved sunshine, like a dog devouring a slab of meat.
          But never really do we stare-
      At those Grass Blades, we don't dare.
    We stride through them, not attaining any sense of life, coming from the tiny sparks of green.
      But on quite a chill of a day,
  I swear I see them dancing, in such synchronization.
    The Sky, looming over the people
But nothing, if ever, a simple "Oh look at the Sky," or possibly, "Wow, the Sky is so pretty today," while we take in the sunset, soaring across the Sky, in several shades.
      Only those who are aware of the true spirits in all our surroundings may stop and see-
        That the Sky's awake, staring at us
regularly, even when it's dark, and we may not detect it.
      It watches down at us, spying on our every move.
        Sometimes, I see a sudden twitch in the Sky,
         Maybe a blink, or an itch in its eye.
      We don't stop and think, is it alive?
    Even the slightest thought that it's not what we saw.
    The Grass Blades, aren't just Grass Blades, the Sky, it's not just-
      a huge blue mass with clouds overheard us.
  How many additional things like these in nature do we deceive ourselves to think we know most about?
    Even though they're all around us, they're yet so far away from our intelligence.

Shriya Vaddigiri, Category F, Plainview-Old Bethpage Middle School, Mr. Reinbold, 2020

Anna Fedotov

"The Making of a Masterpiece"

It all begins with an idea
Or the desire to create.
Then I can improve my own work,
Yet also calmly sit alone

I find the euphoric feeling
From the boxes filled with rainbows,
Pouring water to clean bristles,
And choosing which brush I should use.

I can express and be myself,
Form a moon or make flowers bloom.
I control what goes in and where,
For no one can tell me different.

It all begins with an idea.
Then add the first splotch of color,
Smearing the smooth stuff on the board,
With its rough and scratchy surface.

I would be painting pigment if
Only I had the extra time,
Building beats with the tapping brush
And clanking from whirling water.

It all begins with an idea.
But then like a movie I watch
The piece come together as one,
Bringing me kairosclerosis.

Anna Fedotov, Category L, Mt. Sinai Middle School, Mrs. Wallace, 2020

Grand Champions

2021

"Lessons Learned"

Poet-in-Residence:
Forrest Gander

"Humankind"

I will not be underestimated,
Unequal, compared to all.
On a scale from one to ten,
I will be that ten.
That ten that does not just sit there,
Sit there wondering about kindness,
About equality,
About people, not money.
I will not let them underestimate me,
Or tell me what I can,
Or can't.
I will not just sit there.
I will go out and nurture every moment,
Every moment I am lucky enough to share,
Until I cannot.
And I will say when I cannot.
Not you...or anyone.
Because, according to me,
No one has done their job.
Not until they say they are done,
Or cannot.
Because we are the people of this world,
All humankind,
Of all beliefs, races, genders ... and strengths.

Kelly Shi

"Before Coronavirus"

I remember going to school
the sour smell in science lab
the massive screens in the computer room
the antiseptic smell of the principal's office.
I remember the classroom, where
six kids sat at a table facing each other
the squeak of the teacher's whiteboard
the sound of her voice acting out Alice in Wonderland.
I remember the playground
the hard skin of the bouncy ball
the mounds of tanbark we'd climb on
the kid who fell off the monkey bars.
I remember the cafeteria
the custodian who made us throw trash in the right bin
the cheesy breadsticks dipped in marinara sauce
the bean and cheese burritos.
I remember running to the field with my friends
soft grass grazing on my skin
little white flowers standing like thin sheets of paper
small gopher holes in the field.
I remember the supply box
the smell of the crayons
the blunt-tipped scissors for safety
the broken ends of pencils.
Now, I have Zoom, my room,
a screen full of squares,
books, pieces of paper,
and my memories of what school used to be.

Kelly Shi, Category B; Joshua Chadbourne Elementary School; Teacher: Lisa Bozzo; 2021

Julia Corvea

"Wild Things"

When I was too young to understand
I mistook salt for sugar
When I was naïve, and trusting
My finger lingered on the sizzling pot
They say when you grow older
You're immune to foolishness
But I befriended a fire, for it lit
And ran freely
I befriended a storm, for it electrified
And sent shivers through my spine
I befriended the sun, for it glowed
And loved all life
I befriended you, for your heart
Was gold in deceiving
And soon enough fire burned my sides
My storm electrocuted my spirit
The sun left room for the moon
And you were never there
Now I've learned not to love
Not to try to please
Such wild things
For they are such a thrill
Such a rush of adrenaline
Until you become a wild thing too
Fire belongs in torches
Storms are meant for the deserted
Sun is meant to go down
And you were never mine

Lyla Forest Butler

"Braving Hurricanes"

Lessons learned are like the sky
After a storm of fierce rain and flaming lightning
You must persevere the unbearable
Before everything becomes a little clearer.
Even when the dead of night is silent as a doe
And when the kids laugh in time
With the beat of their angst
And you cry crocodile tears
She comes to you with open arms
Nothing greater than a mother's love

And though the wrinkles in his face
Obscure the once almost barely green of his eyes
His mourning-dove lectures
And the taste of bone broth will never wash out
On the mountainside, the wrinkles instead resemble
Something like a smile as he points out the blue spruce and the moss
That hugs the belly of a bitter stone as you
Admire a grandfather's wisdom

Driving through blurry streets
Unfamiliar, tasteless faces
Arriving in a room full of girls with the voices of
Characters you've heard of before and real people you haven't
So scared and so far from the silver-dollar streets
And loquacious green trees
But as they call your name with-- not vinegar,
But the loudest honey on their tongues
The storm begins to clear
And the umbrellas fold up-- stored away for later
And the sun's rays spill out in a rush
Realizing new friends are not so unlike you after all

Christine Kneuer

"The Life Soon to be Behind"

From a new window
Her life came flooding back.
The scent of the fresh cut grass infused into her clothes
And the mulch that stuck to her feet, staining the carpet as she treads inside
And the fresh cherry blossoms, falling upon her like rain on a May morning
And the sweat, that clung to her forehead like the morning dew on the grass
And the sand that found its way inside, coming from everywhere and nowhere all at once
And the bruises that covered her legs, seemingly coming from the night
And the cuts that mangled her knees, from slipping one too many times from her tree, became part of her.
And the lights of the city, dragging her back to her reality
And the pavement that calloused her feet, leaving nothing but raw skin underneath her
And the mother that comforted her, convincing her that the scrapes and cuts were the only pain she should fear
And the father the realist, that prepared her for the dangers that lay waiting outside her front door
And the walk became part of her, the warm sun and the birds' song and the shimmering grass a stark contrast to the words that filled her ears
And the crying and pain, filling her until she was empty, became part of her.
And the curtains that remained drawn, as to not remind her of the life soon to be behind her, the piano music drifting through the streets, and the sound of childhood surrounding her home that she had not even realized had become part of her, were a part of her.
And the blue front door, standing out against the yellow house fading into the background

And the town that was void of color, all of the light seemingly left behind in a life long forgotten

And the hydrangeas that bloomed, illuminating the world around her, the crash of the ocean bringing back the music that filled the air, and the grass that shimmered as it had when she was a child

And the pavement that cut her, no different from the kind she had left behind

And the house that was no different than before, the blue door setting itself apart form the yellow home, proving that her life left behind was not out of sight.

Christine Kneuer, Category E, Christine Kneuer, Southold High School, Mr. James Stahl, 2021

"Down the Slopes"

When thin air and snow is everywhere.
When you see glistering rocks frozen with ice.
Barren trees across the slopes,
You know that it will be a good day.

My skis glide down the slippery slope,
my legs wobble, my face falls.
I struggle to get back up,
Afraid to fall and break a bone.

I feel sore and breathless trying to rise once more.
Go down the slope
Lose control near a tree
Take time to rest.

But not too long.
I get back up
I do not give up.
I rise and fall.

As the snow swirls in the air
And cold winds swerve through the trees.
Do not stop now
you will succeed.

When the slopes are hard.
I must not stop
I will succeed
I get back up.

Jeffrey Ming Liang

"Cocoon"

With the whistling of the door,
my father appears,
his backpack hanging on his back,
straps embedded into shoulders.
His suitcase strolls obediently beside him,
like a dog inseparable from its leash.
Dressed in a plain checker-pattern shirt,
he glances at me and says, "Alright bye,"
and his light leather shoes lead him out.
A hollow click, and the door embraces the frame,
the floor tiles vibrating in place.
Mother comes after and adjusts her collar,
in the long mirror of the living room.
Her handbag swings on her shoulders,
shifting side-to-side,
and the door creaks and shut.
Her polished high heels hasten her out,
leaving only the shuffle,
of my footsteps scraping the floor
the sporadic bubbling of the water machine,
the random beeping of the rusty fridge.
In an empty cocoon,
I'm neither caterpillar nor butterfly.
But I sit on the couch,
where father reads his miniature books,
where mother watches her favorite Chinese dramas,
where I learn to write in silence.

Grand Champions

2022

"Sing to my soul, renew its languishing faith and hope.."

Poet-in-Residence:
Natasha Trethewey

Riya Golia

The Tree and the Leaves

The tree has beautiful greenery,
dancing in the wind.
Yet
the tree loses its friends
when autumn hits the Earth.
Leaves fall swaying in the wind,
waiting for next summer to be with the tree,
missing each other all alone in the dark night sky.
But
when the sun and rain come back,
the leaves regrow on the tree,
the tree is making new friends.
Yet
it is still missing its old friends and so are they;
the tree is adoring its new beauty loving its new friends,
waiting for next year,
waiting patiently for next year to come,
getting prettier, and prettier,
going through the same cycle
every year.

Riya Golia Category A, Grades 3-4, The Laurel Hill School, Ms. Sorenson, 2022

Alicia DiGiambattista

<u>realization & renewal</u>

re·new·al /rəˈn(y)ooəl/
    1. the feeling of being filled to the brim with motivation. spilling over.
    2. feeling satisfied with where you are, your stage in life.

l. i wake up again.
on any other day i might've been disappointed.
but on this particular morning, something is different.
too old to be new; too new to be old.
something pivotal has gone on inside of me.
two ends meet, i guess you could say is what it feels like.
i'm feeling peculiarly, unexpectedly giddy. renewed, almost.
at first i don't understand it at all.
what am i feeling?

ll. why i was so upset with my life, i don't know the answer.
i guess i just didn't know who i was anymore.
i had morphed into a hard outer shell of someone whom i didn't recognize.
startling, i now recall.
but i notice i'm not just a hard casing anymore. i'm me again. i'm really myself.

lll. i suppose something in me evolved last night while i was busy dreaming,
and my body subconsciously changes.
i change and it was like everything was back in the right place again.
everything that was initially knocked out of place is back. it's refreshing.
what happened, i'm unsure of. . . but something was different
it is exhilarating.
i want things to stay this way.
i want to continue to have the will to live.
i want to be happy like this everyday.
I want to be renewed.

Charlotte Huang

Amongst the Fire

Yesterday the fire roared,
Trees blackened to stumps,
Broken branches lying in ashes,
The forest floor stripped of debris,
The underbrush blazed,
As new land was made,
Unoccupied and waiting.

Today the seeds,
Of lodgepole trees,
Coaxed out of their resistant cones,
Assured by the heat,
Open and release,
Impatient to grow.

Tomorrow the young sprouts earn their first leaves,
Crisp green petals glisten with dew,
Ready for the year anew.

Chloe Lin

Lessons in Farming

      in class we learned about   shifting cultivation—
an agricultural method in which   people shift
 farming from one area to another
       to regenerate the soil

we facetimed to complain   about vocabulary words &
     three-paged speeches   the second time i had ever seen
   your face recognized the green of your walls   hair out of its usual
claw clip   somewhere along our
      slew of sarcastic snorts i realized that

maybe i had   left my land fallow   for a little too long
     bounced between soils   (the boy who wears tank tops
& the boy who bought me boba)
       & nothing has ever grown

     & maybe you aren't meant to   either
but there's something beautiful   about the flowers on your
     kitchen table   translucent stem   crumpled inky purple
thorn brown with water   from the tap

we watched   while they were still red
    silken petals   as if someone had   gone
& kissed them

     we can plant flowers   we can plant whatever
you'd like   anything in this wasteland
    of mine   & this might not be forever
    & i know that   but we can still be beautiful
      a certain kind of beautiful

     flower—   the reproductive structure
of angiosperms   they bloom
when they are exposed to more   sunlight   when ashes have
     washed away & we have blossomed

Thisbe Wu

Shrooms

```
                              Foraging
                       For mushrooms on a cool autumn
                 day. The air dense with humidity. There's something poetic
              about mushrooms in a cemetery. Life springing (in fall) from death, recycled
         matter, all that jazz. As we uproot life from the dirt we craft our own, ready to saute in butter,
           oil, and pepper. Matter cannot be created or destroyed. I learned that from a Justice League
                                       animated series
                                        episode. Isn't all
                                        love recycled?
                                       We drink in the
                                            love
                                          others
                                           give
                                          us &
                                         give it
                                          back
                                         or give                      The largest
                                          it to                 living organism is a honey
             There's nothing             someone             mushroom whose mycelium spans
          More romantic than finding       else.              2384 acres in Oregon. It's grown like
        Your own dinner ingredient beside  "The          m           a web              t
      Herman Melville's grave. The petrichor Love         a            or a         p     o
      s      l      blends     r              You take    k     a      map          r     d
      p      i      with      a    d        is equal     e             of           i     a
      o      k      the       i    r          to the            s      neurons      n     y
      r      e      umami     n    o           Love             p      in the       t
      e             earth          p            You             o      brain,             !
      s             smell          s           Make."           r      for
                      of                    I believe it.       E      2400
                    shrooms                                            Years.
```

Thisbe Wu, Category E, Grade 12, Saint Ann's School, Mr. Marty Skoble, 2022

Kim Standfast

"A Seedling to a tree" from *A New Leaf*

If you plant a seedling,
And watch it grow,
You'll see the changes it goes through,
As roots grow,
Feet on the ground,
ready to rise.
Like a human,
It grows up,
it gets sick,
It makes friends,
Like the bird in the tree,
using the sticks from the tree to make its home.
Or the bunny burrowing in the ground
Making its home in the roots.
Each year,
something new.
someone new.
The tree is as alive as we are.

**Violet Le Claire (author), Emily Gorecki (dancer),
and Jordan Logue (reader)**

phoenix

burning embers have fallen, fallen into the hair of the kids
on the playground, onto the flags hanging outside
the stores in town.
they fell onto my arms and singed my clothes.
i blew on my arms and chest in an attempt to blow
out the flames but the air only spread them.
i try to ignore it but the cafe on the corner erupts
in screams and suddenly i am engulfed.
i don't mind though, it's warm.
the heat is a nice change from the frigid February air.
when the flare dies from my body,
i emerge in what feels like May,
i feel a cool breeze relieving me from the hot weather.
i think i might have died,
but i know
that i am revived

Category L, Grade 12, Walt Whitman High School, Ms. Susan Turner Radin, 2022

Grand Champions

2023

"I am large... I contain multitudes."

Poet-in-Residence: Kwame Dawes

Emily's Poem

you are connected to everything
you are every blade of grass
like every wildflower
you are different from all others
coral, sage, beige, even cobalt blue!
each unique and magnificent
like a kaleidoscope, every individual vibrant shape
takes form to create a masterpiece
like my mother, I am fluent in Chinese
my father's eyes can be seen in my smile
yet, I am not like the others
the talents I possess are uniquely my own
while others fail to draw a flower, I sketch it with ease
while others grumble and complain,
I solve math equations and read contentedly
yet I am not good at everything
while others do sports with ease,
I struggle with the simplest drill.
while others strive to be perfect,
I have learned that perfection does not exist
we are the branches of our community
as different the branches are
and as far apart the branches may be
we are all part of the same tree

Alexeen Dillon

I was Born with Autumn's Leaves

I was born with autumn's leaves
Ever changing like me.

In a way I give air
You will just never see.

Rain pours down with just one hope,
To feed spring's plants and watch them grow.
Yet, you are there providing air for all,
Like me, small things make a difference for all.

As the sun comes up on a hot summer day
It tells kids it is time to play.
But you are exhausted, tired, and deflated.
Like me you push on
For we know we are providing
Something strong.

When winter comes, it says be gone
It puts you down, you are swallowed in its frost
Little do you know, you are being used
Only to do something for the greater good.

The leaves in the seasons
They are ever changing like me
They are there unnoticed, doing something amazing.

We are the colors of life
We are part of a great cycle
We are made up of many multitudes.

I was born with autumn's leaves.

Rebecca Henneman

Untitled

There is no silence anymore
sinking into the deep blue
swimming in your gaze
I do not see them anymore
pulling my arms into your lap
rubbing over my soft skin with your coarse hands
whispering praise
I am trained to long for your voice
laying out on the splintered wood floor
floating in pools of sunlight
dripping onto my body
I don't need you to say you're sorry
nevermind your sullen looks
that ripples fear throughout my skeleton
shaking and shivering because your face says the end
don't make me leave so soon
return to the soft smiles that melt my heart
into a bloody sea
don't throw knives instead
stabbing gashes that rip through the muscle
return to me
return to us

Ava Kuklis

I Am

"Who am I?"
Society awaits a presumably confident response
Collectively bound to a persona, a public image, a reputation, a stereotype
Disregarding spectrum based judgment, you are unknowingly, and uncontrollably perceived
Subject to being falsely translated, vision based judgments you can skew only at eye level

I am a body
Melodies that course through my veins, sound that dictates the beat of my heart
Playing strands of hair like guitar strings, the callus of picking, plucking, fingers
Feet settled above ever changing destinations and evolving terrain
Acrylic scars on arms stretched like canvas, my head painted by Pollock
A pupil of my mother, an iris of my father, a ring of conspiracy bombarding visions of realism

I am an image
Black converse bursting at the sole, my sock easily visible, laces that restrict blood flow
Ripped tights and denim layered beneath stains
The black t-shirts of indistinct bands, worn all too many times
Disguised in an army green cardigan
An identity seen only from an outer shell, little concern for what lies within

I am a distance
Watch from afar, I, a dark, faded figure, a silhouette with blurry borders, think nothing of it
Step closer, clearer, yet insignificant I stand as a person like all
The narrowing space between constructs illusion of individuality, stare into my being
Dissect my imperfections as the gap come to a close, the good the bad the me
Close enough to reach, look but don't touch

I am a time
Birthed into admirable cluelessness, optimism, and innocence
Blind existence makes for malleable potential, fresh youth yet to be polluted by corruption
Growing to fill shoes meticulously crafted with high expectations by those without expectation
Newfound joy in judgment, seeing surroundings through eyes capable of viewing shortcomings
Age opens the blinds to reveal introversion, tormenting self-loathing injected by inheritance
I am incoherent, I am immense, I am immeasurable

house of cards

i am a house of cards. construct me, hear my dimensional whispers.
i shake/fall apart/sprawl on the table as you sort through the faces on those
 cards:
Ho Nansorhon, Chopin, Van Gogh, Hypatia, the fisherman i said hello to last
 weekend.
we all toast marshmallows with Boyle's flamethrower, playing faro.
i am them. they are me. interchangeable parts, invented by Eli Whitney who
 joins us.
the cards are folded into paper planes and i soar, like the airplanes cross-
 stitching
a burnt evening sky flecked with seagull calls. the airplane my parents met
 on. the airplane
embroidering white streamers in the infinite blue prayer. like the lines criss-
 crossing

my palm. each one offering a different permutation of a path in life
but i only get to choose one. and my ancestors pass around the flamethrower to set
their evanescent dreams ablaze, saying *we are the other
 permutations.*
you are the last one but you still get to hold us all in your hand.
press my hand against a window. see the lingering ghost on the glass.

the ghost of my hand that holds the cards that i study with my eyes.
Asian eye/my mother's eye/slim brown eye. anglo eye/my father's eye/wide
    blue eye.
spades and clubs merge, spill out of their own bodies into hearts and
    diamonds. bleed.
on one side of the house is the Twinkie [yellow outside, white inside] on one side of the
house is the egg [white outside, yellow inside]
they face each other through the triangles of the house. they merge, as
    different as 3-D lenses
made of midnight fractals patched together like a stained glass window.
    shards of this
intergalactic cavity we call home. they merge, to make one whole.

i am a house of cards. shuffle me, hear my rippling laughter.
you know me as a deck of cards. but in my splendor
i house myself. i house you. i house the sky, the sea, the ground.
i house the turbulent rip current sloshing beneath my [egg/Twinkie] flesh.
i house history notes, palm readings, smoking marshmallows, soft afternoon
    rain.
i house leaky pens, silent flamethrowers, dissipating music notes.
i house lowercase letters and misplaced, punctuation. i house the black suit
    and the red suit.
i house myself. as a house, i am complete.

Hannah Ninan

Traveling Pots

We are clay, molded to portray living breathing humans
Questioning our existence on a planet out in nowhere
Still made with a purpose-
Perfectly purposely sculpted
As the universe came together to create each one of us.
But those small dents, the exaggerations the sculptor makes - we are those flaws
If we all were perfect, I wonder if we won't need names 'cause we are one,
Molded from the same clay.
Handing over our brokenness, worries, and pressures, to someone out there
To be handed back a beautiful mosaic depicting a story of gold.
We turn into pots carrying golden memories
Together grasping pots of gold we walk on,
Feeling useless but told we are made for greatness.
We carry on to our own rhythm, experiencing a story
None in the billion years of Earth have experienced.
In this pathway, we try to learn the stories of others,
Crossing buildings that hold the minds that could have soared over clouds
   like kites.
Mercy crosses the pink stained glass building
Through which the grandness of the illuminations falls on the faces of sinners.
We go through the highs and lows of life, waiting in line to become stable,
So to finally rest in peace and be happy in solitude.
Sweet solitude, like an oasis
Though we crave solitude,
In multitudes, we are born, we walk, we die.
Though seasons change, our fight doesn't seem to stop,
We fight together to endure the coldness of our hearts and the heat of our minds.
Fighters, we are, fighting that these rains and storms don't deform us.
Though death brings peace, we fight to make it out happy with our way of life.

sixth period

the boys' bathroom smells like
chemicals and smoke
and i am in a gravestone of life
i am waiting for the fire alarm to ring
spray me with the holy water on the floor
refresh me with the sense of the high school
where am i in this moving set piece
where do i fit in here
or is this desk simply too small for me
the crushed vape pen on the floor
is still fuming, still waiting
for someone else to submit to the galaxy
handing over fate for the gods of detention
kiss me with your breath
it smells like corporate greed
lock the door and turn down the lights
mop the floor and start a fight
you are waking up slowly
and when you realize that we are all dust
i wonder where all that gravitas will go
i wonder where all the slurs you use will go
i wonder how your thoughts will dissipate
into gasses infused with nicotine
and i wonder just how many birds
they will kill in the process

Christina Pan

Tiny Allegiances from Whispers Across the Fields

Mom held my hand through the smoky streets, through the faceless drivers
    behind their unlit windows.
I skipped as she walked, reciting the tale of the monkey from school.
I dream of the day you can tell me your story in English, she said.

Lofty, I thought, like she told me to climb up to the clouds and
Invite the angels down to play gorillas in a tea party.

Giants walk the earth, walk past me, forever a third grader.
In my sleep I pledge my loyalty to my age, a patriotic third grader.
Yet every year my pledge changes, tacking on just another year,
Writing just another name, displaying just another photo.

My tongue faded while strange sounds came in as replacements.
My song, my poems, my letterbox, ripped from me slowly like

I was deaf to the tears of the pages until the pages are lost to the western winds,
Blown to oceans away, soaked, dissolved, its ink washing away.

Malia Lockhart

My Hair That Makes Up Me

My hair is a multitude of me.
My hair is chestnut brown like the mahogany Swietenia Macrophylla trees That sway graciously in Africa.
My hair has kinky, curly strands that tell stories of their own.
My hair is a way to convey my instinctive state of mind.
I wear my hair as a crown,
A way to project myself abstractly rather than verbally.
I wear my hair in twists when I feel like holding in my emotions, forming rows Like cornfields being grown in the golden-dipped sky.
Sometimes I wear my hair in puffs when I'm ecstatic,
Two ponytails that defy gravity,
round like the planets that orbit the sun in the anonymous star-speckled sky.
I wear my hair out, kinks, curls, and all, freely expressing themselves
With no designated destination,
For I wear my metaphoric crown like this when I am in a state of tranquility.
At times I wonder if my hair is too much, Too loud?
Too expressive?
Too excessive?
Yes,
My hair may be all these things, maybe my hair is eccentric, It may not fulfill today's rigorous system of beauty,
But it's mine.
Mine to express my perplexed feelings to the world,
Mine to tell my story, Mine to wear.
My hair is a crown that shines like a beacon. My hair is beautiful,
My hair is a multitude of me.

Malia Lockhart, Category L, Grade 8, Munt Sinai Middle School, Mrs. Wallace, 2023

Malia Lockhart, Category L, Grade 8, Munt Sinai Middle School, Mrs. Wallace, 2023

Paige Sweeney

There is Time

As the assignments flow in,
As the responsibilities are present,
As the anxiety takes control,
I have no time, I have no time.

The minutes pass while I stare at a molecule
The minutes pass as I sit, exhausted from my day
The minutes pass as I worry about my due dates
The minutes pass as I perfect every answer
The minutes pass as I long for more time.

Yet,
There is time,
There is time for laughter
There is time for joy
There is time to watch the koi circle in the flowing pond.
There is time for perseverance
There is time for rest
There is time to see sunrise and sunset
There is time for care
There is time for growth
There is time for running hand in hand with the ones you love most
There is time for food
There is time for plants
There is time to give creativity a chance
There is time to bake
There is time to read
There is time to walk amongst the trees
There is time to live your life.

I have time, I have time.

Paige Sweeney, Category L, Grade 12, Oyster Bay High School, Dr. Faughey, 2023

Index

Alzafarani, Noor	130	Fedotov, Anna	136
Amazan, Nathalie Esther	100	Fitzsimons, Kyle	76
Andrews, Jonathan	37	Flanagan, Greta	124
Aneziris, Eleni	92	Golia, Riya	146
Barry, Nathan	106	Gorecki, Emily	152
Biancaniello, Jennifer	77	Gozaloff, Katie	116
Bowers, Michelle	14, 21	Graffeo, Daniella	118, 127
Brathwaite, Christine	19	Gravitz, Emily	154
Brennick, Chase	3	Hackenberg, Ariana	5
Brett, Bailey	111	Hafeez, Amani	94, 101
Burke, Tessa	104	Halbohn, Chris	13
Butler, Lyla Forest	141	Heiman, Arielle	47
Burney, Izyaan	131	Henneman, Rebecca	156
Chang, Tiffany	55	Huang, Charlotte	148
Cheng, Jocelyn	82	Huang, Crystal	86
Choi, Jenny	15	Jiao, Tiffany	126
Ciringione, Erica	49	Kayel, Chris	46
Conroy, Phaedra Damianos	73	Kelly, Lizette	102
Corvea, Julia	140	Kennedy, Trevor	53
Daniel, Christina	29	Khan, Summar	66
Davis, Boone	112	Kies, Gregory	98
DeFeo, Dylan	48	Kirkpatrick, Bailey	28
Derasse, Ryan	123	Kneuer, Christine	142
De Vito, Ryan	34	Kocay, Eloise	58
DiBennardo, Justin	54	Kokolakis, Kara	114
DiGiambattista, Alicia	147	Kuklis, Ava	157
Dillon, Alexeen	155	Kumar, Muskan	105
DiNorcia, MaryKate	32	Lau, Carolyn	133
DiPietro, Diana	8	Lazzaro, Dominique	59
Doherty, Sean	30	Le Claire, Violet	152
Dove, Brandon	36	Levitin, Miriam	67
Eggleston, Jade	125	Lewis, Sarah	117
Fan, Carly	134	Leybov, Hadar	107
Farrell, Jonathan	12	Li, Melvin	68

Liang, Jeffrey Ming	144	Scott, Isabelle	45, 91
Lin, Chloe	149	Seidel, Micheal	4
Liu, Linda	42	Shi, Kelly	139
Lockhart, Malia	165	Silver, Kenny	80
Logue, Jordan	152	Soto, Evelyn	96
Lu, Hannah	72	Spiegel, Jos	33
Luo, Ashley	81	Spotorno, Matteo	128
Marquart, Krisann	26	Spotorno, Tatianna	85
Martinez, Cristian	121	Stancampiano, Lindsay	93
McDonnell, Claire	39	Standfast, Kim	151
Metcalf, Elena	65	Strauss, Jack	64
Moll-Rocek, Thomas	24	Sun, Kate	122
Montemurro, Klye	69	Sweeney, Paige	167
Morgenthal, Sarah	90	Sweeney, Terrence	62
Morrone, Casey	27	Sweetman, Emily	56
Muessig, Colin	89	Takvorian, Sophia	108
Murphy, Katriel	115	Taylor, Courtney	75
Nichitiu, Marc David	97	Testa, Micheal	18
Ninan, Hannah	161	Turnier-Baez, Tristan	61
Niven, Jack	52	Vaddigiri, Shriya	135
Olsen, Rina	159	Wallace, Allison	40
Oreste, Philip	71	Wang, Tianru	84
Osswald, Neve	138	Wanlass, Brooke	23
Pan, Christina	163	Weinstein, Alec	41
Pasca, Rainer	162	Wu, Alanna	88
Perdue, Brighton	143	Wu, Thisbe	150
Pioli, Adriana	113	Yu, Dorothy	60
Ramos, Christian	109	Zhang, Ray	132
Rand, Violet	79		
Raposo, Laura	16		
Rewkowski, Lia	120		
Ross, Amy	43		
Ryan, Kevin	6		
Sagarino, Jordan	33		